THAT'S NOT FAIR

THAT'S NOT FAIR

A Program for
Teaching Catholic
Social Doctrine
to Sixth Grade
and Up

THIRD EDITION

**THOMAS TURNER
AND PATRICIA HANEY**

SAINT MARY'S PRESS®

Dedicated to our parents, William and Alice Turner and Robert and Ruth Scherrer, who by their example taught many people about God's love.

Genuine recycled paper with 10% post-consumer waste. 5111800

The publishing team included John Vitek, development editor; Lorraine Kilmartin, reviewer; Mary Koehler, permissions editor; pre-press and manufacturing coordinated by the prepublication and production services departments of Saint Mary's Press.

Printed in the United States of America

Printing: 9 8 7 6 5 4 3 2 1

Year: 2014 13 12 11 10 09 08 07 06

ISBN-13: 978-0-88489-916-7
ISBN-10: 0-88489-916-0

Library of Congress Cataloging-in-Publication Data
Turner, Thomas.
    That's not fair : a program for teaching Catholic social doctrine to sixth graders / Thomas Turner and Patricia Haney.— 3rd ed.
        p. cm.
Includes bibliographical references (p.   ).
ISBN 0-88489-916-0 (pbk.)
    1. Christian sociology—Catholic Church—Study and teaching. I. Haney, Patricia. II. Title.
BX1753.T88 2006
268'.432—dc22
                                                        2005033448

CONTENTS

PREFACE

I would yell "SHOTGUN!" as my brother and I, as kids, walked to our parents' car. The unwritten rule among kids is whoever calls "Shotgun" first gets to sit in the front seat. Even if I called it out first, my brother ran ahead and sat in the front seat. I would then appeal to my parents with the simple yet forceful plea, "That's not fair!"

Children cry out "That's not fair" in many situations. Younger children say it when they have to go to bed earlier than their older brothers and sisters. Teenagers say it when their parents won't let them see an R-rated movie when all their friends can. Teachers hear it when their students think the homework assignment is too extensive, the test is too hard, or the grade received is too low.

Children, when they feel they have been slighted in the least, are quick to call out, "That's not fair." Although their plea may be voiced without knowing the whole picture, they are to be commended for being so sensitive toward injustices.

Their cry, "That's not fair," typically refers to a rule or policy that they feel is being ignored or unjustly applied to them.

When I told my parents it wasn't fair that my brother grabbed the front seat after I "called" it, I was telling them that he ignored an agreed-upon rule for his own benefit. When children complain it's not fair that their bedtime is earlier than their older brothers' and sisters', they are saying the rule or policy about bedtime is not uniform.

Children are quick to sense situations that seem unfair. And they are quick to speak up about it. It's a sensitivity and outspokenness that most adults have lost along the way.

Obviously there are greater injustices in the world than who gets to sit in the front seat of a car or what time one has to go to bed. We are aware of injustices like slavery, discrimination, child labor, torture, abject poverty, abortion, and many other issues.

Fortunately for those who suffer injustices, the Catholic Church has a very keen sensitivity and a willingness to shout out, "That's not fair." Popes and bishops have spoken and written about injustices around the world for decades. Their writings about these injustices make up what is commonly known as Catholic social doctrine.

Catholic social doctrine, briefly stated, is the Church's way of critiquing societal structures, laws, and customs with the values of the Bible and the Church's traditions. Like children, Church leaders keep watch for written or unwritten laws, societal structures, and customs that are unjust.

Unfortunately, Catholic social doctrine has not been taught or read by many, and has been called "the best-kept secret" among American Catholics. U.S. bishops, in their concern for this lacuna in Catholic teaching, challenged Catholic educators in 1998 to increase awareness of the doctrine. In *Sharing Catholic Social Teaching: Challenges and*

Directions, the bishops urged Catholic educators and administrators to create additional resources and programs that address the lack of familiarity with Catholic social teaching among educators and students.

This program, titled *That's Not Fair,* is a response to the bishops' challenge. The purpose of this program is to teach the core concepts of Catholic social teaching. These concepts include the dignity of the human person, the difference between charity and justice, solidarity, subsidiarity, and a preferential option for the poor. The program is most appropriate for sixth and seventh grade students, but may be adapted for eighth grade students.

This program is also designed to teach parents and the adults in your parish and school through the students. The students will make a presentation to the adults about the basic principles of Catholic social teaching and how it applies in a practical case.

—Thomas Turner

INTRODUCTION

Learning Objectives

That's Not Fair is designed to provide students with fun, interactive, and high-quality education that reflects the beliefs of the Catholic Church. After completing this program, students should be able to do the following:

- Understand why some individuals live in poverty and why others do not

- Describe the Catholic Church's teaching on human dignity, respect for human life, and preferential protection for those who are poor and vulnerable

- Understand the concepts of subsidiarity, solidarity, and human equality

- Understand socioeconomic factors affecting persons and families in today's climate

- Describe the purpose of social service agencies and how they work to help those in poverty

- Choose to make a difference in the lives of others who are less fortunate

- Coordinate a campaign to change laws or policies that discriminate against those in poverty

Teaching Catholic Social Doctrine to Children

The Teaching Circle

The heart of this course is the Church's teaching on human dignity. Appropriately, this teaching is put at the center of the diagram.

Next, the course teaches other principles of Catholic social doctrine through activities, games, and parables. The students participate in a classroom activity and try to discern the meaning of the activity.

After the students have some conceptual knowledge of the Church's teaching, as it relates to people who are poor, they will meet with people who are living in poverty. Ideally this should take place in a social service agency. This setting alone communicates to the children a message of responding to human needs.

Next, working with appropriate Church organizations, the leaders of the program will help the students identify an issue to which they can apply the Church's teaching.

The students will then give a presentation to the adults in the parish, at either a Sunday Mass or an evening function at the parish. Finally, the students will perform some action on behalf of justice, such as meeting with a legislator.

Parables

When I was in grade school, I would ask my parents the meaning of a word, and their response was always the same: "Look it up." A dictionary graced our house at all times. It would have been much easier for my parents to just tell me what the word meant, but they knew I would retain its meaning if I had to put forth some effort.

I read a line not long ago that went like this: "I forgot everything I was taught. I remembered everything I learned." It's a great aphorism for all educators. Students learn better when they "discover" meanings, rather than being "spoon-fed."

In the Gospels, Jesus tells lots of parables. A parable is a short story with a hidden message that the listener is invited to discover. It says in the Gospel of Matthew, "All these things Jesus spoke to the crowds in parables" (13:34).

Jesus, as a good teacher, wanted his students to learn by discovery.

The classroom activities in this course are ostensibly simple games. Yet underneath each game—or parable, if you will—is a hidden message. As a presenter, you are to present the parable and assist the students in discovering its message.

Program Adaptations:
Can this be used in a school of religion setting?

Yes; however, you'll have to make some adaptations.

The program was originally designed in and for a traditional Catholic grade school setting, where the students are coming Monday through Friday throughout the day. As there are nineteen lessons in the program, it is not that difficult to work them in the regular religion curriculum. However, nineteen lessons in a parish religious education setting would take up almost the whole course, which may not be practical.

I would suggest working in whatever classroom lessons you can. The M&M's game is easy to do and teaches many valuable lessons. I would do this one for sure and whatever other ones you think are important and have the time to do.

Visiting a social service agency may not be possible. Many agencies close by 5:00 p.m., and you simply will not be able to do this. If not, the next best solution would be to see if an agency could have one of their clients come and visit and give their testimony to the students. I have taken some of our agencies' clients to the classroom, and it has worked out fine. (See lesson 9 on how to handle this session.) If that is not possible, you may have to be satisfied with the *Wishing I Were a Princess* video as a way to help the students understand the reality of poverty. This 14-minute video presents testimonies from children in homeless shelters. (It can be obtained from Coleman Advocates for Children and Youth for a free-will donation by calling 415-239-0161.)

The part of advocating in front of a legislator might prove to be the biggest challenge. The purpose of this part of the program (lessons 17 and 18) is to give the students an experience of doing justice. I am sure some legislators would make themselves available in the evening, especially when they know the students have been studying a particular issue. I would recommend that you ask the legislator to wear professional dress, whether they come in the evening or during the day. By their dress you want them to communicate to the students that they take them and their message seriously.

If getting a legislator to come in person proves too difficult, you could always have the students write letters to their representatives. Obviously this doesn't have the same experiential learning as an actual visit.

Good luck!

Seven Principles of Catholic Social Teaching

The Church's social teaching is a rich treasure of wisdom about building a just society and living lives of holiness amid the challenges of modern society. Modern Catholic social teaching has been articulated through a tradition of papal, conciliar, and episcopal documents. The depth and richness of this tradition can be understood best through a direct reading of these documents. In these brief reflections, we wish to highlight several of the key themes that are at the heart of our Catholic social tradition. At the front of each unit plan are several quotations from Church documents and the Scriptures that provide a grounding in Catholic social teaching for the lessons. The bibliography at the end of the book offers good ideas for learning more.

1. Life and Dignity of the Human Person

The Catholic Church proclaims that human life is sacred and that the dignity of the human person is the foundation of a moral vision for society. Our belief in the sanctity of human life and the inherent dignity of the human person is the foundation of all the principles of our social teaching. In our society, human life is under direct attack from abortion and assisted suicide. The value of human life is being threatened by increasing use of the death penalty. We believe that every person is precious, that people are more important than things, and that the measure of every institution is whether it threatens or enhances the life and dignity of the human person.

2. Call to Family, Community, and Participation

The person is not only sacred but also social. How we organize our society in economics and politics, in law and policy directly affects human dignity and the capacity of individuals to grow in community. The family is the central social institution that must be supported and strengthened, not undermined. We believe people have a right and a duty to participate in society, seeking together the common good and well-being of all, especially those who are poor and vulnerable.

3. Rights and Responsibilities

The Catholic tradition teaches that human dignity can be protected and a healthy community can be achieved only if human rights are protected and responsibilities are met. Therefore, every person has a fundamental right to life and a right to those things required for human decency. Corresponding to these rights are duties and responsibilities to one another, to our families, and to the larger society.

4. Option for the Poor and Vulnerable

A basic moral test is how our most vulnerable members are faring. In a society marred by deepening divisions between people who are rich and people who are poor, our tradition recalls the story of the Last Judgment (Matthew 25:31–46) and instructs us to put the needs of those who are poor and vulnerable first.

5. The Dignity of Work and the Rights of Workers

The economy must serve people, not the other way around. Work is more than a way to make a living; it is a form of continuing participation in God's creation. If the dignity of work is to be protected, then the basic rights of workers must be respected: the right to productive work, to decent and fair wages, to organize and join unions, to private property, and to economic initiative.

6. Solidarity

We are our brothers' and sisters' keepers, wherever they live. We are one human family, whatever our national, racial, ethnic, economic, and ideological differences. Learning to practice the virtue of solidarity means learning that "loving our neighbor" has global dimensions in an interdependent world.

7. Care for God's Creation

We show our respect for the Creator by our stewardship of creation. Care for the earth is not just an Earth Day slogan; it is a requirement of our faith. We are called to protect people and the planet, living our faith in relationship with all of God's creation. This environmental challenge has fundamental moral and ethical dimensions that cannot be ignored.

This summary should be only a starting point for those interested in Catholic social teaching. A full understanding can be achieved only by reading the papal, conciliar, and episcopal documents that make up this rich tradition.

(These principles are summarized from *Sharing Catholic Social Teaching,* by the United States Conference of Catholic Bishops [USCCB], pages 4–6.)

Advocacy

Social justice is about taking action to effect systemic change, more than a particular social project such as organizing a food or clothing drive. This program concludes, therefore, with students advocating to legislators on behalf of people who are poor on an issue they are concerned about. Children need to know how to advocate. It's up to us to teach them.

Getting Started

1. Enlist your key players.

- *Pastor.* The pastor needs to be supportive of the program. At a minimum he is asked to let the students make a presentation at a weekend Mass (usually in February or March is what is recommended in the program) on what they have learned about Catholic social teaching and how it applies to a particular issue. The presentation is usually less than 5 minutes. The more the pastor is engaged with the process and the issue, the better the success of the program.

- *Principal (or director of religious education if used in a parish setting).* The principal needs to be supportive of the program. The principal should be instrumental in identifying someone (probably from the parish) who would be the "outside presenter" (see below).

- *Teacher.* The teacher needs to take ownership of the program and hopefully have some empathy for people who are poor. The teacher needs to be "hands-on," not a mere observer, when the outside presenter is in the room.

- *Outside presenter.* We have found the program works best with a volunteer who helps the teacher. The teacher could do the program without such assistance, but a fresh face brings energy into the classroom and emphasizes the importance of the program. It is similar to the D.A.R.E. program that has an officer come into the classroom to talk about drug abuse. The outside presenter needs to have a desire and some natural ability to teach young people. He or she needs to be sensitive to people who are poor, and ideally volunteers or works with people who are poor. He or she needs to have passion for social justice. He or she needs to be available during school hours, as his or her presence is required in the classroom about one class period every two weeks from October through mid-March. (See appendix A for a sample job posting for the outside presenter.)

- *Social service agency contact.* A key part of the program is when students listen to a low-income person give testimony about poverty's oppression. Therefore, either the teacher, the outside presenter, or the overall coordinator needs to set this up with a willing social service agency. Ideally the exchange should be done at the agency so that the students can see how it operates. If this kind of "field trip" is too inconvenient, the low-income person may come to the school.

- *Someone who will pick the social justice issue to work on.* This task could fall to a number of people: the pastor, the principal, the teacher, the outside presenter, the parish's peace and justice office, or the diocesan peace and justice office.

- *Overall coordinator.* If more than one school in a diocese is using this program, it will necessitate having an overall coordinator. The main tasks of the overall coordinator are to keep all the schools on track, to line up the visits to the social service agency, to identify and research an appropriate issue, and to line up the legislators and venue where the advocacy will take place.

2. Provide program supplies for a class of thirty students.

You will need:
- a folder in which each student can store program papers and notes

For lesson 1
- a deck of playing cards
- bags of peanut M&M's (each bag contains approximately 21 pieces), sufficient quantities so that each "rich" student receives a whole bag and each "poor" student receives two M&M's pieces
- eight to ten envelopes, depending on the size of the class, with prizes (for example, actual items students can use, such as cash or gift certificates to video rental stores or area restaurants)

For lesson 2
- *If I Were a Princess* video, available from Coleman Advocates for Children and Youth, San Francisco, CA, 415-239-0161, *www. colemanadvocates.org.*

For lesson 4
- six large balloons
- papier-mâché (choose one of the following techniques):
  - flour, water, and newspaper
  - wallpaper paste, water, and newspaper
  - papier-mâché mix purchased at a craft store (one package per balloon)
  - plaster casting material (You may have a parent in a health profession who can donate this.)
- six large bowls
- six strips of poster board

For lesson 5
- several colors of tempera paint
- paintbrushes
- glitter, ribbons, sequins, pipe cleaners, feathers, and so on

For lesson 11
- thirty fabric loops (cloth strips or pieces of yarn approximately six feet in length)

For lesson 12
- two hundred feet of clothesline rope

For lessons 15 and 16
- fifteen pieces of poster board

3. Plan in advance.

The advanced planning of this program is lining up a social service agency to work with and choosing an issue that your students will eventually advocate for to legislators. As is outlined in the upcoming pages, this planning ideally is taken on by someone who has the time and the connections to make this happen. Normally I do not see this as a role for the teacher or principal.

4. Notify parents and enlist their support.

Before you begin the program, it's a good idea to send a letter home with your students telling their parents about *That's Not Fair*. Some of the homework assignments require parental help.

There may be some resistance from some parents. This program is intended to educate both children and adults about Catholic social doctrine.

Lesson Plans

The lesson plans in this book contain complete instructions for classroom implementation. While you are building your students' knowledge of Catholic social doctrine, you will also be building their teamwork skills, as each lesson contains structured and integrated teamwork activities. Feel free to adapt the lesson plans to meet your students' needs and your curricular goals.

Each lesson plan begins with a theme. Church teachings and biblical quotes are provided for you as background for the unit. The lesson begins with an activity, continues through a discussion of the activity, and often concludes with a homework assignment that leads to a discussion.

Leapfrog Classes

Lesson 9 involves going to a social service agency. If an agency cannot accommodate you during the time this session is planned, leap over lessons 9 and 10 (lesson 10 is a follow-up to lesson 9) and pick up at lesson 11. Then complete lessons 9 and 10 when your agency visit is scheduled.

UNIT ONE

Justice

Theological Background: "Which one do you love most?"

Let's begin.

A friend of mine is the mother of six children. I asked her, which one of her kids does she love the most? Her head jerked back and her face scrunched as if to say, "What a stupid question." Her eyes teared a bit and she said, "Why, I love them all the same."

No doubt this mother and her husband have to settle many disputes among their six children. Each child has a different set of needs and gifts. Often these needs and gifts conflict with those of another. One child needs to get to soccer practice at the same time that another needs to be picked up from a friend's house. The parents do their best to meet each child's needs and maximize each child's gifts.

When disputes arise among their children, sometimes parents must deny one child her or his need for the sake of the other. The parents make these decisions not out of spite or hatred, but out of love. A good parent cannot do otherwise. When this mother of six settles disputes or makes compromises among her children's needs, she is practicing justice.

Justice is love practiced in complex situations. Charity is the practice of love to alleviate an immediate need, often toward an individual. Helping your child with his or her homework is charity. Justice looks more to rules, policies, systems, or structures (for example, the setting of "house rules" so that everyone in the family is considerate of the needs of others). "No loud playing of music on a school night" could be one.

By and large, Americans are good at charity. We are good about responding to individuals' needs. Food pantries, soup kitchens, and the Red Cross are all examples of charity at work. This follows from a philosophy focused on individuals. Justice, responding in love to complex situations, is more difficult for most Americans to grasp. Tax laws, economic policies, and international trade all affect the quality of life for many people. Sorting out the fairness of laws, policies, and social structures is a tougher act.

God sees all humans not only as equal but also as connected. Like this mother of six, God loves all, because all are God's children. It is this vision of love that drives the biblical sense of justice. We share our resources with the needy because we see them as family.

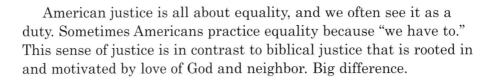

American justice is all about equality, and we often see it as a duty. Sometimes Americans practice equality because "we have to." This sense of justice is in contrast to biblical justice that is rooted in and motivated by love of God and neighbor. Big difference.

Bible Quotes

Defend the lowly and fatherless;
    render justice to the afflicted and needy.

(Psalm 82:3)

To do what is right and just
    is more acceptable to the LORD than sacrifice.

(Proverbs 21:3)

The LORD loves justice and right
    and fills the earth with goodness.

(Psalm 33:5)

For the LORD loves justice
    and does not abandon the faithful.

(Psalm 37:28)

    Learn to do good.
Make justice your aim: redress the wronged,
    hear the orphan's plea, defend the widow.

(Isaiah 1:17)

"Woe to you, scribes and Pharisees, you hypocrites. You pay tithes of mint and dill and cummin, and have neglected the weightier things of the law: judgment and mercy and fidelity. [But] these you should have done, without neglecting the others." (Matthew 23:23)

"Behold, my servant whom I have chosen, my beloved in whom I delight; I shall place my spirit upon him, and he will proclaim justice to the Gentiles." (Matthew 12:18)

Church Documents

Charity will never be true charity unless it takes justice into account. Let no one attempt with small gifts of charity to exempt himself from the great duties imposed by justice.[1]

(USCCB, *Economic Justice for All,* no. 120)

It grows increasingly true that the obligations of justice and love are fulfilled only if each person, contributing to the common good, according to his own abilities and the needs of others, also promotes and assists the public and private in situations dedicated to bettering the conditions of human life.

> (Pope Paul VI, *Gaudium et Spes*, no. 30)

Man's relationship to his neighbor is bound up with his relationship to God; his response to the love of God, saving us through Christ, is shown to be effective in his love and service of [men]. Christian love of neighbor and justice cannot be separated. For love implies an absolute demand for justice, namely a recognition of the dignity and rights of one's neighbor.

> (Synod of Bishops, *Justice in the World*, no.34)

Biblical justice is more comprehensive than subsequent philosophical definitions. It is not concerned with a strict definition of rights and duties, but with the rightness of the human condition before God and within society. Nor is justice opposed to love; rather, it is both a manifestation of love and a condition for love to grow.[2]

> (USCCB, *Economic Justice for All*, no. 39)

"In order to overcome today's widespread individualistic mentality, what is required is *a concrete commitment to solidarity and charity*, beginning in the family."

> (Pope John Paul II, *Centesimus Annus*, no. 49)

Lesson 1: M&M's Game

Learning Objectives

- The students will be able to describe the difference between charity and justice.
- The students will be able to explain why we should share our gifts with others—because God created us all and has blessed us with gifts.
- The students will understand that as a result of God's creation, each person enjoys special dignity.

The purpose of this introductory activity is to provide students with background knowledge of social justice, and to understand that there is a difference between charity and justice.

Preparation

1. Prepare the materials for the lesson. You will need a deck of playing cards, twelve regular-sized bags of peanut M&M's, envelopes containing prizes equal to the number of face cards used in this exercise, and a bag to hold the M&M's.

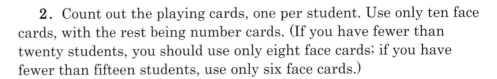

2. Count out the playing cards, one per student. Use only ten face cards, with the rest being number cards. (If you have fewer than twenty students, you should use only eight face cards; if you have fewer than fifteen students, use only six face cards.)

3. Copy the homework assignment.

4. Meet with the outside presenter to familiarize yourself with the lesson.

The Lesson

The teacher should begin the lesson by introducing the outside presenter and telling the students that she or he wants to play a game with them. Allow some time for each student to introduce herself or himself to the presenter. You may want to consider having the students wear name tags.

Instructions for the Presenter

1. Pass out a playing card to each student, saying "I am going to give each of you a card and you may not look at it until I tell you to."

2. After you have passed out the cards, tell the students to look at their cards. Then arrange the seating into two rows so that those with a face card are on one side of the room and those with a number card are on the other side of the room.

3. Tell the students that those with face cards are "the royalty" and those with number cards are "the lowly number people."

4. Initiate a discussion with these questions:
- "What is it like to be a person who is poor?" Amplify and affirm responses. For example, if a student says, "They probably don't get many toys at Christmas," respond by saying: "That's a good answer. Our parish does a toy drive each year for kids who otherwise wouldn't get any toys."
- "What do you think of when you hear the words *poor person?*" Amplify and affirm responses. Anticipate that students may describe a dirty, drunken, homeless man.

5. Pass out the M&M's. Give two pieces to each person who is poor (those with a number card), and a whole bag to each person who is rich (those with a face card). Tell the students not to eat the M&M's or open the bags until you tell them to.

6. Tell the students about the prizes:
- "Each of these envelopes contains a prize. You can buy these prizes, or 'gifts,' from me today." Tantalize the students by telling

them the contents of some of the envelopes. Help them picture themselves enjoying the gifts. After they see the value of each gift, ask the students what they think they will use to buy the gifts and how much they think each gift will cost.

7. Explain the rules of the game:
- Each gift costs eighteen M&M's.
- Since the lowly numbers have only two M&M's, tell them they will have a chance to get more M&M's by asking the royalty to share with them: "Don't worry; you'll get a chance to get more M&M's. You will be asking the royalty to share with you. You need to start thinking of reasons why the royalty should share their M&M's with you."
- Tell the royalty: "You can do whatever you want with your M&M's. You can eat them, take them home, share them, or use them to buy prizes. When they, the lowly numbers, come begging, it is up to you to decide whether you listen to them or not."
- When the lowly numbers ask the royalty to share, they must get on their knees. (This simulates the indecency of poverty.)
- Gifts cannot be split between the lowly and the royalty. (It's possible that someone on the poor team is a good friend of a person on the rich team. He or she may say, "Give me yours and we'll split the gift certificate to the movies." However, in the real world, the rich are not taking the poor out to a movie.)
- The rich team may buy a gift at any time: "You don't have to wait for the people who are poor to beg you for M&M's. Buy what you want, when you want."

8. Tell the students not to open the envelopes until all the gifts are purchased. Be ready to begin handing out the envelopes as students come forward with eighteen M&M's. Give the class a signal to begin. Have a bag ready, as students will "pay" for a gift by placing eighteen M&M's in the bag.

9. After all the gifts have been purchased, ask the students to return to their seats.

10. Tell them, "That's the end of the game." Then, initiate a discussion with this question:
- "What were the messages of this game?" Listen for: "People only share after they get what they want, not need." "God decides which families we are born into." "It hurts to beg." "Some have more than others." "The rich have easier access to gifts." "It's a game about sharing." "It's a game about greed."

Ask the students to describe the type of sharing that did take place. What you are listening for is a description of "leftover sharing," that is, we tend to share with those who are poor after we have made sure all our needs and wants have been fulfilled. You may tell the students who did "leftover sharing" not to feel bad, as that is how most adults share. Most people do not donate to the point that they no longer have enough money to go to the movies or out to eat. "Leftover sharing" describes what probably takes place when schools or parishes conduct food drives.

11. Ask the questions:
- "Should those with more share with those who have less?" Most students will say yes.
- "Why should those who have more share?"

This is a critical question. It is disarmingly simple, but even adults have had a hard time answering this question when I have played the M&M's game with them. This question is looking for motives of giving. Many people, when pressed for an answer, will disclose their motive as one that is self-serving or in their self-interest. For example, some have said, "It makes me feel good to give." Or, "I might be poor one day, and if I help a person who is poor now, maybe someone will help me." One adult actually said, "If we don't share with those who are poor, they will revolt against us (the rich)." The other motive for giving is religious in content. For example: "God made us all." "Because Jesus said we are to share." "We are all brothers and sisters in the eyes of God."

Throughout the program you will want to emphasize Christian motives of charity and justice for sharing or helping others. It is important to teach the students the right thing to do as well as the reason for doing so. For example, we conduct a food drive in our school, and the students may be rewarded for achieving a certain goal. We forget to tell them that this is a way of showing our love for others who are in need, which is our Christian duty.

12. Ask the children to hold up their cards and say: "See how we are different? Some of you are black fours. Some of you are red sevens. Some of you are kings and queens."

13. Talk about any social differences you are aware of; for example, in many cities, ethnic groups often live in the same part of town, as do people of similar income levels.

14. Direct the students to show the back sides of their cards, and ask them, "What do you see?" Listen for: "We are all the same." "God doesn't see color or rich or poor. He sees only sons and daughters."

15. Ask the students who they think you represented at the beginning of the game when you passed out the cards. They should guess "God." And that's right. Explain that passing out the cards at the beginning of the activity symbolizes the differences that exist

between us and is part of God's plan, who wills that we help each other. He distributes his gifts among us unequally so that we need each other.

16. Ask the students, "What were the rules of the game?" You might even write them on the board. Then ask, "Were the rules fair?" They should say, "No." Ask, "How could the rules be more fair?" Listen for: "Change some of the rules." "Give everyone the same amount of M&M's."

17. Explain and emphasize the two ways the Church says we can help people:
- *Charity.* Direct assistance, such as giving the people who are poor more M&M's. Explain how charity is like a food drive.
- *Justice.* Changing unjust rules, such as lowering how much the prizes cost. Explain that this program is about justice, about learning how to help people change unjust rules.

18. Pass out the homework assignment on handout 1. Ask the students to illustrate two of the three concepts from this lesson. The three concepts are:

(1) a person who is poor

(2) an act of charity

(3) an act of justice

Anticipate that most students will opt not to illustrate an act of justice, because it is a concept that most Catholics are not familiar with; hence, the purpose of this program.

HOMEWORK

Name:_____

Draw two pictures, one on this side of the sheet, and one on the other side. Illustrate two of the following three ideas:

_ 1. a person who is poor

_ 2. an act of charity

_ 3. an act of justice

Check the box by the two ideas you are going to illustrate.

Lesson 2: Wishes

Learning Objective

The purpose of this activity is to gain a more accurate understanding of the people who are poor in our country. Most people think the "poor" are men who beg on the street. Yet, the truth is that most people who are poor are women and children.

Preparation

1. Prepare the materials for the lesson. You will need a television and a videocassette player to show the video *If I Were a Princess.* You also will need file folders (if you want the students to keep the program papers together).

2. Label the file folders with the students' names.

The Lesson

1. Ask the students to have their homework assignments on their desks. (As an option, collect the homework assignment beforehand and make transparencies of some of the drawings in preparation for today's discussion.)

2. Review the lessons from the M&M's game:
- We don't choose the families we are born into.
- Those with ample resources have easier access to material goods.
- It doesn't feel good to beg.
- Typically, people will give from their "excess" to the needy, but keep enough so they can get what they want.
- The difference between charity and justice is that charity is giving something specific, say a hot meal, to an individual, where justice is changing a law or social structure to benefit many.
- The rules of the game represent social structure.

3. Initiate a discussion about the homework assignment, using the following questions:
- "Who wants to show her or his picture of a person who is poor?" "How did the person in your picture get this way?" "Can you make up a story to go with this picture?" Continue the discussion using more pictures.
- Ask the students to share their pictures with another student. "Do they look the same?" "Who drew a man?" "Who drew a man with ragged clothes?" "Who drew a man without a home?"
- "Who would like to share his or her drawing of an act of charity?" "How do you think the person or people in your picture feel?" "Why

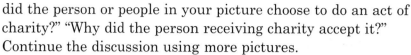

did the person or people in your picture choose to do an act of charity?" "Why did the person receiving charity accept it?" Continue the discussion using more pictures.

- "Did anyone illustrate an act of justice?" Chances are, not many students did, because an act of justice is much harder to illustrate. "Why is this an act of justice and not charity?" "What was the result of this act of justice; what change took place?"

4. Place the drawings in the individual folders.

5. Before introducing the video ask the students to write down one wish they have in life. Have the students take 15 to 30 seconds to share their wish with someone sitting near them. Then say, "Now that you have your wish written down, we are going to watch a video that will help us begin to understand what living in poverty is like."

6. Show the video.

7. Initiate a discussion after watching the video, using these questions:
- "How did your wishes compare to the wishes of the kids in the video?"
- "How did your picture of a person who is poor compare to the pictures of the people who are poor in the video?"

The discussion should reinforce the objective of this lesson to gain a more accurate picture of people who are poor.

UNIT TWO

Human Dignity

Theological Background: "Who Made Me?"

In the old *Baltimore Catechism,* the first question was, "Who made me?" The simple three-word question was followed by a three-word answer, "God made me."

There is a solid theological reason why this is the first question of the *Catechism.* The Church understands the human person as a special creature of God. God breathed life into humans, an action he did not take with the rest of creation. Humans carry the breath of God.

Therefore, we are special. As the current *Catechism* says, the human person is "the only creature of earth that God has willed for its own sake[3]" (no. 1703).

This theological understanding of the human person is different from a secular understanding. Secular anthropology avoids metaphysics; therefore, it does not speculate on the origins of humans beyond biology. Likewise, it does not speculate on the end of humans beyond death. Not only does the Church teach that we began with God, but that we end with God, too. That is, the Church believes that humans have a life beyond this earthly one.

A secular understanding of the human person leads to an ethic that is based on self-interest, pragmatism, or utilitarianism. These are ethical systems that promote actions that primarily benefit the self, as opposed to others.

What does a secular ethic look like? Take an example from a Catholic school. Some students may bring in canned food for a food drive just so that they can receive some sort of reward for meeting a goal. That is, we help others so that we can get something. Although collecting food for people who are poor is a good thing, doing it for a self-serving motive represents an ethic based on self-interest. Self-interest is a secular ethic.

How is this different from a theological ethic? Take the same example and change the motive.

A Christian ethic of collecting food for people who are poor reflects the truth that the same God created me and my poor neighbor in his image and likeness. Jesus, God's Son, has shown us the way of life that is rooted in an obligation to do what is good because we are followers and imitators of him. We are, therefore, brothers and sisters in Christ, children of the One God. This represents an ethic that is rooted in faith and centered in actions that reflect the kind of love Jesus taught. The difference between a Christian ethic and a secular ethic is not a small thing.

This course teaches that we are children of God, that all people are made in the image and likeness of God—they carry the "breath of God" within—and that we do good for others because we are followers of Christ. That is why we help others.

Even if no other point is communicated to the students during this course—besides the Church's understanding of the human person—the course will be a success.

Bible Quotes

The LORD God formed man out of the clay of the ground and blew into his nostrils the breath of life, and so man became a living being. (Genesis 2:7)

Thus says the Lord GOD to these bones: See! I will bring spirit into you, that you may come to life. (Ezekiel 37:5)

"Whoever has my commandments and observes them is the one who loves me. And whoever loves me will be loved by my Father, and I will love him and reveal myself to him." (John 14:21)

You formed my inmost being;
   you knit me in my mother's womb.

(Psalm 139:13)

Can a mother forget her infant,
   be without tenderness for the child of her womb?
Even should she forget,
   I will never forget you.

(Isaiah 49:15)

Before I formed you in the womb I knew you,
   before you were born I dedicated you,
   a prophet to the nations I appointed you.

(Jeremiah 1:5)

"And the king will say to them in reply, 'Amen, I say to you, whatever you did for one of these least brothers of mine, you did for me.'" (Matthew 25:40)

Church Documents

This Council lays stress on reverence for the human person; everyone must consider one's every neighbor without exception as another self, taking into account first of all life and the means necessary

to living it with dignity,[4] so as not to imitate the rich man who had no concern for the poor man Lazarus.[5]

(Pope Paul VII,
Gaudium et Spes, no. 37)

The basis for all that the Church believes about the moral dimensions of economic life is its vision of the transcendent worth—the sacredness—of human beings. The dignity of the human person, realized in community with others, is the criterion against which all aspects of economic life must be measured. . . . When we deal with each other, we should do so with the sense of awe that arises in the presence of something holy and sacred. For that is what human beings are: we are created in the image of God. (Gen 1:27)

(USCCB, *Economic Justice for All,* no. 28)

"Man . . . is the only creature on earth which God willed for itself."[6] God has imprinted his own image and likeness on man (cf. Gen 1:26), conferring on him an incomparable dignity. . . . In effect, beyond the rights which man acquires by his own work, there exists rights which do not correspond to any work he performs, but which flow from his essential dignity as a person.

(Pope John Paul II, *Centesimus Annus,* no. 11)

The human person is the clearest reflection of God's presence in the world; all of the Church's work in pursuit of both justice and peace is designed to protect and promote the dignity of every person. For each person not only reflects God, but is the expression of God's creative work and the meaning of Christ's redemptive ministry.

(USCCB, *The Challenge of Peace,* no. 15)

Lesson 3: Creation

Learning Objectives

- The students will express their understanding that God makes human persons.
- The students will discuss their understanding that human dignity is a result of being created in the image and likeness of God.

Preparation

1. Be prepared to divide the class into six workable groups. Students will work together in these groups for the rest of the program.

2. Prepare for the lesson by making six copies of handout 2, "Creation," so that each group will get a copy. Also make a copy of handout 3, "Homework: Talents and Gifts of a Human Person," the homework assignment for each student.

2

The Lesson

1. Review what was learned from the M&M's game, asking: "What was the message you learned from the M&M's game?" "What did you learn from the video?"

2. Divide the class into six groups. Tell the students, "We want to see which group can come up with the longest list of things that are in the Creation stories of the Bible."

3. Distribute a copy of handout 2 to each group.

4. Allow 5 minutes for each group to brainstorm and record their ideas on one sheet.

5. Allow time, 20 to 30 minutes, as a class to share some things from the groups' lists.

6. Read the following story of Creation from the Bible to the class, saying, "This is one of the stories from the Bible about the creation of humans":

When the LORD God made the earth and the heavens—while as yet there was no field shrub on earth and no grass of the field had sprouted, for the LORD God had sent no rain upon the earth and there was no man to till the soil, but a stream was welling up out of the earth and was watering all the surface of the ground—the LORD God formed man out of the clay of the ground and blew into his nostrils the breath of life, and so man became a living being. (Genesis 2:4–7)

(The entire Creation stories can be found in the first three chapters of Genesis.)

7. Tell the students: "Imagine that when God created animals, he used a huge mixing bowl. What ingredients, or qualities, would God have poured into the mixing bowl to make a lion?" Listen for things like speed, strength, a heart, some roar. "What ingredients, or qualities, would God have poured into the mixing bowl to make an elephant?"

8. Continue the discussion: "Again I want you to imagine what ingredients God put into the mixing bowl to make the human person."

Listen for things such as love, free will, intelligence, an ability to communicate, laughter, tears, and a soul. Then ask these questions:
- "Why do you think he breathed into this mixture but not the other mixtures?"
- "What kind of breath do you think God used? Did he blow softly or hard? Why?"
- "Why did God decide to create humans last of all creation?"

9. Direct the groups to use the back of handout 2 to write out a list of the qualities, talents, gifts, spiritual powers, and passions (for example, love) of a human person.

10. Explain to the students that they will need to think of a symbol for each talent or gift that can be placed in their human person. They are to think of small objects that can be placed inside the person that symbolize each talent or gift. To fit into the human persons they will make, the symbols should be no bigger than a fist.

For example, a picture of one's friends symbolizes friendliness or love. A lightbulb symbolizes intelligence. A tennis ball symbolizes athleticism. The symbols should be objects, not pictures or drawings of an object. Each student will be responsible for bringing to class one or more symbols. Let the students know that these symbols should not be things of lasting value or family treasures, because there is the risk of something being broken or misplaced.

11. Distribute copies of handout 3, "Homework: Talents and Gifts of a Human Person." Allow time for the students to copy talents and gifts from their group list onto their homework papers. Go over the directions with the class, and encourage the students to enlist the help of others (for example, parents, grandparents, siblings). Be sure to tell the students that they are to bring back symbols of talents or gifts that were brought up in class and some they would come up with at home.

CREATION

Group Members

Name: _____   Name: _____

Name: _____   Name: _____

Write down anything you remember from the "Creation" story.

HOMEWORK: TALENTS AND GIFTS OF A HUMAN PERSON

Name: _____

My group compiled the following list of qualities that we feel are unique to a human person. These qualities make humans different from the rest of God's creations:

_____   _____   _____

_____   _____   _____

_____   _____   _____

Think of symbols that can be placed in your "human person" that will represent each quality. You can use some or all of the qualities listed above, and you can add other qualities that your group did not think of.

Quality Symbol
Here's an example: intelligence = lightbulb

These people helped me:

_____   _____   _____

Lesson 4: In God's Image

Learning Objective

The purpose of this activity is to create a symbol of the "human person." The students will take a blown-up balloon and cover it with papier-mâché. When completed, each "human person" will be about the size of a basketball.

Preparation

1. You will need one balloon per group of students, papier-mâché mix, newspaper, large bowls for the papier-mâché, and six strips of poster board for bases.
- papier-mâché (Choose one of the following techniques.)
  - flour, water, and newspaper
  - wallpaper paste, water, and newspaper
  - papier-mâché mix can be purchased at a craft store (one package per balloon)
  - plaster casting material (You may have a parent in a health profession who can donate this.)
- a strip of poster board about 3 inches wide by 12 inches long

2. Before the lesson, prepare the papier-mâché mix according to directions. Join each end of the poster board paper strip so it forms a circle, and staple the ends together so it serves as a stand.

3. Review and familiarize yourself with the lesson outline on the following pages.

The Lesson

1. Review the story of Creation read in lesson 3, on page 30. Remind the students that in the story of Creation, God breathed life to create humans. Tell them that in this lesson, "you will create an image of the human person in a similar way by blowing air into your balloon to give it shape and form."

2. Divide the class into the groups they were assigned to in the last session.

3. Give each group a balloon and direct them to breathe into it until it reaches its full size.

4. Have the students cover their balloons with the papier-mâché mix. Caution the students not to cover the balloon near the knot. They need to leave an opening about 4 or 5 inches in diameter so they can put symbols inside it.

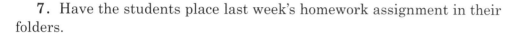

5. When the students are finished, place the balloons on the poster board bases and allow them to dry.

6. Ask the students to look at their homework from the last session. Ask them, "What symbols did you write down?" Tell the students that for the next session, they are to bring the physical objects that are their symbols. You may want to allow them to bring the objects to school any day before the next session. (The symbols must be small enough to fit into the hole at the top of the balloon, and not of any value.) You'll want to provide a safe area to store the symbols.

7. Have the students place last week's homework assignment in their folders.

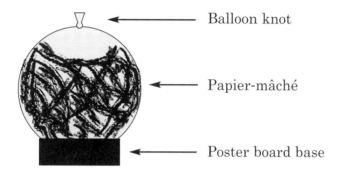

Balloon knot

Papier-mâché

Poster board base

Lesson 5: Faith, Hope, and Love

Learning Objective

The purpose of this activity is to decorate the symbols of their "human person" in a way that reminds the students that the human person is filled by God with three virtues: faith, hope and love.

Preparation

1. You will need several colors of tempera paint, newspaper (for the workspace), paintbrushes, decorations (for example, glitter, ribbon, feathers) appropriate for decorating their "human persons," and the six poster board strips.

2. Review and familiarize yourself with the lesson.

The Lesson

1. Gather the class again into their groups and have them prepare an adequate space to put their "human persons" together.

2. Tell the class that they are going to decorate the outside of their "creations" in such a way that their human person would stand out among all creation. Remind them of these points:
• "This is a symbol of a human person."

- "The symbol of your human person should be decorated so that the opening is at the top. The 4-to 5-inch hole needs to be at the top of the balloon, as you will later put things inside your person."

3. Provide necessary materials: balloons, papier-mâché, and items for decorating, and allow time for the groups to decorate their human persons as they wish.

4. Tell the students: "Now that we have decorated the images of our persons, we want to make them into a community. We will want to have a community of human persons, much like we have here in our school or our town."

5. Calling on one group at a time, allow each group to share the names and ages of all the human persons in their community. Explain to the groups that they will now spend some time decorating a new base for their community of human persons.

6. Hand each group a poster board strip. Tell the students that names and ages of all the people in their symbolic community should be prominently displayed in a bold fashion on the bases so they will be easy to read from a distance.

7. Display the finished symbols of their persons in the classroom.

Lesson 6: Community Making

Learning Objective

The purpose of this activity is to encourage a sense of responsibility for the human persons by making them into a community.

Preparation

Review and familiarize yourself with the lesson. The outside presenter will return to class to meet the community of human persons. Review the lesson with the outside presenter.

The Lesson

1. The presenter should ask about the created persons: "How did you make them?"

2. Ask the students to share the symbols they have collected for their created persons. Encourage them to state a quality that matches each symbol. Have the students place the symbols in the person through the hole.

3. Ask each group to describe its human person, inside and out. Ask why they decorated their creations the way they did, why they put the symbols in that they did, and why they gave them a particular name.

4. Praise each group profusely. You want to foment the pride they have in their "creations." Talk about the core message of this experience: "God took a long time to make a real person. Part of God is in each of us. All of us contain valuables."

5. Draw a table on the chalkboard, as illustrated below, with three columns and two rows. Leave enough space in each box of the table to write in the responses from students.

Body	Growth	Injure
Soul	Growth	Injure

6. Ask the students to give you examples of things that help the body grow, things that injure the body, things that help a human person grow, and things that injure a human person. Make the lists as long as you want.

7. Choose one of the human person creations and talk about the ways the students said you could injure it. Then take a pair of scissors and cut away a small piece of one of the papier-mâché creations. The group who made that particular "human person" will likely react with dismay.

8. Ask them how they felt when you did this. Ask them why it would be wrong to do this to a human person. You might ask them to begin their statements with these words, "God, would say it is wrong because . . ." This begins to teach them about the dignity of the human person. For example, it is wrong to injure another person because God created it with love.

9. Ask the students how God would want us to heal any injury we cause to another human person. Ask them to begin their responses with these words, "God, would . . ." This helps them reflect on how God might want human people to interact with one another, in reconciliation and forgiveness. They may say things like, "God would tell us to treat each other as we want to be treated."

10. Ask the students how God talks to human persons. Lead them to see how God works through other people—like them. The students should begin seeing all people as human beings created and loved by God. Furthermore, when we see an injured human person, we may be moved by God to help bring comfort and healing, justice and charity.

UNIT THREE

A Decent Life

Theological Background: "It's our nature to rise."

Submarines can go only so deep in the water. At a certain depth, the pressure is too great and they will collapse like aluminum cans in a crusher.

Water cannot stay a liquid if the temperature drops too far. Below 32°F, water becomes a solid.

Airplanes cannot keep flying under certain speeds. If a plane goes too slow, it stalls and drops out of the sky.

Nature sets "minimums." A thing dies, crashes, changes its nature, and in general, is in trouble when it goes below its minimum.

Humans are susceptible to nature's minimums. Too little air and we would suffocate. Too little heat and we would freeze. Too little water and we would dehydrate.

There are other minimums below which humans are in danger. These are minimums that have to do with our dignity.

Humans require a certain amount of respect. If a human does not get a minimal amount of respect, he or she is in danger. To be pushed down or disrespected is against our nature because God wills that all people be respected.

Humans need to have enough food to eat, enough heat to be warm in the winter, enough clothes to wear, enough work to make a living, enough means to provide for their children, enough time for leisure, enough love, and enough time to pray. Any less than this is unbecoming of a human.

A human living without enough food, warmth, clothing, work, leisure, love, and prayer falls below nature's minimums. Like a submarine that goes too deep, the human is in danger of collapse. Every human, made in the image and likeness of God, ought to have a "decent life": a life that never goes below certain minimums.

Anytime we see a human living below the minimum, we ought to help lift her or him up.

Many of our brothers and sisters around the world live below the poverty line. The phrase *poverty line* is another way of saying "decency line" or "nature's minimums." People who live below this line are in danger and in need of help. Regardless of how they got there, we must help them get above the poverty line so that they may be able to live a life of dignity.

Bible Quotes

"Because they rob the weak, and the needy groan,
    I will now arise," says the LORD;
    "I will grant safety to whoever longs for it."

(Psalm 12:6)

Though I am afflicted and poor,
    the Lord keeps me in mind.
You are my help and deliverer;
    my God, do not delay!

(Psalm 40:18)

For the LORD hears the poor,
    does not spurn those in bondage.

(Psalm 69:34)

He who oppresses the poor blasphemes his Maker,
    but he who is kind to the needy glorifies him.

(Proverbs 14:31)

Woe to those who enact unjust statues
    and who write oppressive decrees,
Depriving the needy of judgment
    and robbing my people's poor of their rights.
Making widows their plunder,
    and orphans their prey!

(Isaiah 10:1–2)

The afflicted and the needy seek water in vain,
    their tongues are parched with thirst.
I, the LORD, will answer them;
    I, the God of Israel, will not forsake them.

(Isaiah 41:17)

And look at the guilt of your sister Sodom: she and her daughters were proud, sated with food, complacent in their prosperity, and they gave no help to the poor and needy. (Ezekiel 16:49)

Church Documents

The human person is the clearest reflection of God's presence in the world; all of the Church's work in pursuit of both justice and peace is designed to protect and promote the dignity of every person. For each person not only reflects God, but is the expression of God's creative work and the meaning of Christ's redemptive ministry.

(USCCB, *The Challenge of Peace*, no. 15)

But when necessity has been supplied, and one's position fairly considered, it is a duty to give to the indigent out of that which is left over.

(Adapted from Pope Leo XIII, *Rerum Novarum*, no. 22)

It is necessary also that governments make efforts to see that insurance systems are made available to the citizens, so that, in case of misfortune or increased family responsibilities, no persons should be without the necessary means to maintain a decent standard of living.

(Adapted from Pope John XXIII,
Pacem in Terris [Peace on Earth], no. 64)

The [worker's] remuneration must be enough to support the wage earner in reasonable and frugal comfort.

(Adapted from Pope Leo XIII, *Rerum Novarum*, no. 34)

[Development] is not only a question of raising all peoples to the level currently enjoyed by the richest countries, but rather of building up a more decent life through united labor, of concretely enhancing every individual's dignity and creativity, as well as his capacity to respond to his personal vocation, and thus to God's call.

(Pope John Paul II, *Centesimus Annus*, no. 29)

The family "requires balance. Without leisure there is too little time for nurturing marriages, [and] for developing parent-child relationships."

(Adapted from USCCB, *Economic Justice for All*, no. 337)

Human freedom is often crippled when a [person] encounters extreme poverty, just as it withers when he indulges in too many of life's comforts and imprisons himself in a kind of splendid isolation.

(Pope Paul VI, *Gaudium et Spes*, no. 31)

Material deprivation . . . seriously compounds such sufferings of the spirit and heart.

(USCCB, *Economic Justice for All*, no. 86)

Indeed hunger for education is no less debasing than hunger for food: an illiterate is a person with an undernourished mind.

(Adapted from Pope Paul VI, *Populorum Progressio,* no. 35)

Lesson 7: Preparing a Budget

Learning Objectives

- The students will develop a budget that would enable a family of six to live a decent life.
- The students will describe what it means to live a decent life and identify those things that are required for a decent life.

The purpose of this activity is to provide students with an understanding of how much money it generally takes for an average family of six to live a decent life. The core message is that people who live in poverty live "indecently."

Preparation

1. Prepare for the lesson. You will need a transparency of the "Decent Life Line," as shown below (or you can draw it on the chalkboard), and a list of budget questions.

2. Prepare the homework assignment. Complete the necessary information for the letter to parents and the list of budget questions. Copy the letter and questions so that each student has a set. Write a student's name on each one. There are fifteen questions. For a classroom of thirty students, each child will estimate the answers to two questions with help from his or her parents. Highlight two questions on each sheet, being careful not to assign two difficult questions to one student.

The Lesson

1. Begin by reviewing what the students learned about creating their persons. Ask them: "What did you learn when making your human persons? What did you learn about injuring others?" Direct them to write down one or two sentences about what they have learned so far in this class.

2. Invite the students to share their statements. Make notes of the statements. These can be used to help the students get started with their presentation later in the program.

3. Ask the students to define what they think the term *a decent life* means. (A decent life means at least a minimum of physical comforts and necessities: enough food, shelter, warmth, and safety. A decent life means respect—physical or verbal abuse would be contradictory. A decent life is one that is not extravagant or luxurious but has enough resources that are becoming of a human.)

3

4. Introduce today's lesson: "Today we're going to talk about what it takes to live a decent life . . . all the things a family needs. Now remember, we are talking about needs, not wants. A family may want a TV or a phone in every bedroom, but that is not a need or a necessity."

5. Draw a horizontal line on the board or on a transparency on the overhead. Label it "Decent Life," then say: "If a family is living above the line (point to the area above the line), it has all the things it needs. Depending on how far the family is above the line, it has quite a few extras, too.

"If a family is living right on the line (point to the line), it has all the things it needs, but nothing more.

"If a family is living below the decent life line (point to the area below the line), it doesn't have any extras, nor does it have all the things it needs to live a decent life.

"What are some necessary ingredients for a decent life?"

As the students brainstorm needs, list them on the chalkboard or overhead transparency. Listen for things such as a house, heat (gas), food, clothes, a pet, personal items, a car, water, insurance, gifts, a phone, air conditioning, electricity, furnishings, children's activities, a vacation, and entertainment.

Then ask the students, "Of the things you identified, which things are necessary for a decent life and which things might be extras—nice to have but not necessary?" You might have to add some of the things the Church teaches are necessary for a decent life that the students did not identify.

6. Hand out the parent/guardian letter (see sample on handout 4) along with the parent/guardian handout (handout 5), and the budget questions for discussion at home (handout 6). Have the class fill in the ages of the children in the directions on the budget questions.

Then say: "You are going to work on this with one of your parents. You will need her or his help to decide how much each item will cost a family of six for one month. You only need to answer the questions on your paper that are highlighted. Remember, it is only an estimate about an imaginary family of six. We don't want to know what your family spends." (You might have to emphasize this latter point. You don't want a student going home telling a parent, "My teacher wants to know what our house payment is each month.")

Be sure the students have the assignment over a weekend to allow parents the time they may need. Advise the students of the due date (next week's session). Encourage them to bring the assignment back anytime before that date and place it in their folder.

SAMPLE LETTER TO PARENT OR GUARDIAN

Dear Parent or Guardian,

As part of our *That's Not Fair* program, your child's class has created a ficticious family.

The class has decided that they want their family to live a decent life. A decent life means a minimum of physical comforts: enough food, shelter, warmth, and safety. A decent life means respect: physical or verbal abuse would be contradictory. A decent life means one that is not extravagant or luxurious but has enough resources that are becoming of a human.

Attached to this letter is information about the Church's teachings on Catholic social doctrine.

With your assistance, the class is going to develop a budget that would enable their family to live a decent life. Please help your child answer the two highlighted questions. He or she needs only an estimate, not how much your family spends on the items.

This assignment is due on _____, but may be sent back to school anytime between now and then.

Thanks so much for sharing in this experience with your child. We'll let you know the results!

Sincerely,
(Teacher's name)

PARENT OR GUARDIAN HANDOUT

Why Are Humans Special?

The human person is the clearest reflection of God's presence in the world; all of the Church's work in pursuit of both justice and peace is designed to protect and promote the dignity of every person. For each person not only reflects God, but is the expression of God's creative work and the meaning of Christ's redemptive ministry.

(United States Conference of Catholic Bishops,
The Challenge of Peace, number 15)

How Should Humans Live?

"For no one ought to live other than becomingly."[7]

(Pope Leo XIII, *Rerum Novarum,* number 22)

No persons should be without the necessary means to maintain a decent standard of living.

(Adapted from Pope John XXIII,
Pacem in Terris, number 64)

The Church is solicitous for the requirements of the people in their daily lives, not merely those relating to food and sustenance, but also to their comfort and advancement in various kinds of goods.

(Adapted from Pope John XXIII, *Mater et Magistra,* number 3)

Families should have enough to live in reasonable and frugal comfort.
(Adapted from Pope Leo XIII,
Rerum Novarum, number 22)

. . . enough to properly maintain a family and provide for its future.

(Adapted from Pope John Paul II,
Laborem Exercens, number 19)

[Development means] building up a more decent life . . . of concretely enhancing every individual's dignity and creativity, as well as his capacity to respond to his personal vocation, and thus to God's call.

(Pope John Paul II, *Centesimus Annus,* number 29)

The family requires balance. Without leisure there is too little time for nurturing marriages, and for developing parent-child relationships.

(Adapted from the United States Conference of Catholic Bishops, *Economic Justice for All*, number 337)

What Happens When Humans Do Not Live Decently?

Human freedom is often crippled when a [person] encounters extreme poverty, just as it withers when he indulges in too many of life's comforts and imprisons himself in a kind of splendid isolation.

(Pope PaulVI, *Gaudium et Spes*, number 31)

Material deprivation . . . seriously compounds such sufferings of the spirit and heart.

(United States Conference of Catholic Bishops, *Economic Justice for All*, number 86)

Indeed hunger for education is no less debasing than hunger for food: an illiterate is a person with an undernourished mind.

(Adapted from Pope Paul VI, *Populorum Progressio*, number 35)

What Does Our Church Say?

Our Church says everyone ought to be able to have a life that:
• is decent
• is comfortable (within reason and frugal)
• is properly balanced
• includes some leisure
• is "becoming" of a human

QUESTIONS FOR DISCUSSION

For a family of six (a mom and dad with four children ages _____ and residing in _____), how much would it cost to live a decent life?

1. How much would the food bill be for a month?

2. How much would the house payment be for a month?

3. Averaged over a year, what would be the monthly gas bill?

4. Averaged over a year, what would be the monthly electrical bill?

5. On average, what would be the monthly water bill?

6. Averaged over a year, what would be the monthly phone bill (including long distance)?

7. How much would the family spend on vacation and entertainment each month? (Divide your yearly estimate by 12 to obtain a monthly average.)

8. How much would this family spend on clothes each month? (Divide your yearly estimate by 12 to obtain a monthly average.)

9. How much would it cost to have a pet, such as a dog, for a year? (Divide your yearly estimate by 12 to obtain a monthly average.)

10. How much would they spend on personal items (for example, toiletries, haircuts) in a month?

11. How much would the car or cars cost each month (including insurance, maintenance, gas, and wear and tear) or how much would public transportation cost each month? (Divide your yearly estimate by 12 to obtain a monthly average.)

12. How much would this family spend a year on activities for the children (for example, team sports and other activities)? (Divide your yearly estimate by 12 to obtain the monthly average.)

13. How much would health insurance, medical bills, life insurance, prescriptions, and dental insurance be for this family for a year? (Divide your yearly estimate by 12 to obtain a monthly average.)

14. Approximately how much would it cost each year to maintain a house or apartment for this family? (Include replacing or repairing broken appliances, furniture, toys, bicycles, lawnmowers, painting, heating and plumbing repairs, and so on.) (Divide your yearly estimate by 12 to obtain the monthly average.)

15. How much would this family spend on gifts for others each month (including charitable contributions)?

16. How much would this family pay in taxes each month (including income tax, property tax, or other taxes associated with their household)?

Lesson 8: The Cost of a Decent Life

Learning Objective

- The students will estimate the budget necessary for a family of six to live a decent life.

The core purpose of this lesson is to help the students understand that people who live in poverty do not have enough money for life's basic necessities. Therefore, they do not have the resources for the "decent life" God wills all people to have.

Preparation

1. Prepare for the lesson. There is a budget sheet included with this lesson. Either draw it as best you can on the board, or copy it to a transparency and use it on an overhead. Each student should have their completed homework assignment in hand.

2. Calculators will be used to average student estimates.

The Lesson

1. Begin by introducing the lesson: "You have all worked with your parents to estimate some of the living expenses necessary for a family of six to live a decent life. Please have your budget questions and answers out on your desk."

Average the responses you receive from all the students that complete each respective question. Ideally you'll have at least three answers to each question. Record the answers on the spreadsheet on the overhead transparency or on the chalkboard, depending on which approach you prefer.

2. Ask the students: "Let's start with the first question. How much would this family's food bill be for a month? Raise your hand if you were assigned that question."

3. Continue asking about each item, and record their answers on the spreadsheet in estimate columns.

4. Then say: "Now let's find the average monthly food bill. You will need to use your calculator to add the estimates and then divide by the number of estimates. We need to round our average to the nearest dollar." Allow time to average estimates. You should also be using a calculator to compute averages.

5. Record the amount in the average column. Continue with the rest of the questions in the same manner.

6. Then say: "Now that we have the averages for each expense, how can we figure out the total dollar amount necessary for a family of six to live a decent life?" Follow the steps below, asking the students to help compute the estimated monthly cost of living a decent life. Complete the calculation on the chalkboard or an overhead so that all the students can see.

- Add the averages for each expense.
- Allow time for the students to compute.

"So . . . we have estimated that each month it would cost about $_____ for a family of six to live a decent life!"

7. Ask the students, "Using our monthly average, how can we find out how much money our family would need each year to live a decent life?" (Multiply monthly average by 12.)

8. Write the yearly dollar amount on the "Decent Life" line.

9. The purpose of this exercise is to give the students some idea of a family budget. Not many sixth graders would have any concept of how much it takes for a family to have the bare necessities. Tell them that if a family of six makes $5,000 less than the figure you came up with, they probably struggle financially, but manage to get by.

However, if a family makes $10,000 or $20,000 less than the "Decent Life" amount, they are probably living "indecently." It helps the students understand, to the extent that they can appreciate, the poverty line. When they visit with a low-income person at the social service agency in a future session, and hear how little that person makes, this exercise will give them some context to make sense out of that figure.

10. Have the students place their budget questions back in their folders.

11. Let the students know that soon they will be visiting a social service agency to meet some clients there. They will also have lunch or a snack while they are there. (You may want to prepare permission slips.)

AVERAGE YEARLY INCOME ESTIMATES CHART

EXPENSE	ESTIMATE 1	ESTIMATE 2	ESTIMATE 3	ESTIMATE 4	AVERAGE
Food bill					
Natural gas					
Electricity					
Water					
Gifts					
Telephone					
Vacation and entertainment					
Clothing					
Pet					
Personal items					
Car(s)					
Children's activities					
Insurance					
Furnishings					
Total					

_____   x   _____   =   _____
monthly   total months   yearly total

_____   x   _____   _____
minimum wage   hours/weeks   yearly salary at minimum wage

UNIT FOUR

Subsidiarity

Theological Background

"I can do it myself!" This is a common complaint children often direct toward their parents. At certain ages, children no longer need help from their parents, whether it is tying their own shoes for the first time, doing their homework, or figuring out a puzzle. They feel more grown up when they do it on their own.

When a child complains, "I can do it myself," she or he is calling her or his parents to practice what the Church calls the "principle of subsidiarity." Subsidiarity is letting those who are under you make their own decisions when intervention "from above" is unnecessary.

At the heart of the principle of subsidiarity is respecting others as fellow creations of God who have the right to express themselves. The opposite of subsidiarity would be dictatorship; that is, someone who is in charge telling others how they are to think and act.

The Church, in its social doctrine, asks governments to practice subsidiarity. (It is mainly aiming its sights on socialistic governments when making this request.) The principle of subsidiarity, though, is not one that is meant just for government officials; it has applications in many social settings. Parents need to let their children be creative. Teachers need to encourage student participation. Supervisors and managers need to give their employees the freedom to innovate. People who are rich need to respect the ideas of those who are poor.

People in power are tempted to control those who are under them. Those without power tend to be resentful when their creativity or freedom is unfairly stifled. People in power are tempted to think that they know what is best for those under them—even without asking for those people's opinions. People without power often feel ignored. Subsidiarity, if nothing else, is a call for increased communication between those who are in power and those who are powerless.

Again, the principle of subsidiarity is recognition of the dignity afforded to each and every person, no matter how powerless he or she may be. It is to see the other as God sees him or her. Practicing subsidiarity is possible when we see the other person as he or she really is: a child of God.

Breaking Poverty Stereotypes

I was returning to work one morning when I saw a man in disheveled clothes standing by a stoplight holding a cardboard sign. His sign read, "I need food. I am <u>VERY</u> hungry." He had capitalized and under-lined the word *very*.

I rolled down my window and asked, "Do you want some food?" He said, "Yes." I said: "This is your lucky day. I run a pantry up the street. Hop in." He got in. As we drove the half mile to our social serv-ice agency, I asked him what kind of response he gets from people as he stands at that stoplight. He said, "Some give me a little money, others curse me."

I asked, "How do you feel when people curse you?" He said: "It's all right. They don't know me or what I've been through."

Many people who are poor come to our social service agency for food. I don't know them all, let alone know what they have been through. There are as many reasons for economic poverty as there are people who are poor. They all have their own story.

Here are some of the causes of poverty I have distilled from their situations: physical disability, mental disability, elderly with no pen-sion and little social security, having a "deadbeat dad" who doesn't pay child support, school dropout, inadequate schools, employers who can't or won't pay a living wage, tragic upbringing, drug abuse, inabil-ity to "network" for a good job, extended family can't or won't help, lack of motivation, discrimination, lack of public transportation, tak-ing care of a disabled family member, taking care of small children, greedy people, unexpected illness, no health care or health care insur-ance, and unmarketable skills.

Those who cursed the man holding the sign probably think this guy's poverty is his own fault and therefore not deserving of help. That may be true. But as you can see, there are many reasons for poverty, and most of them are not the fault of the person who is poor.

I have yet to meet the person who chose poverty. It's not an easy lifestyle. People who are poor typically live in substandard housing, have no telephone or car, rely on pantries where the amount and kind of food received is not their decision, wear used clothes, and can't afford to put their kids on sports' teams.

The ethos of the television show *Survivor* is to get rid of the weak "tribe members," because the last one standing wins a million dollars. The ethos of the Bible is to keep everyone on the island and to lend a hand to the weakest. Saint Paul uses the image of a body with many parts—some are feet, some are heads—yet all are part of the same body. Seeing all humanity as "connected" is at the heart of the Church's teaching on giving preference to people who are poor. Those who are poor are a part of me.

Bible Quotes

Jesus summoned them and said to them, "You know that those who are recognized as rulers over the Gentiles lord it over them, and their great ones make their authority over them felt. But it shall not be so among you. Rather, whoever wishes to be great among you will be your servant; whoever wishes to be first among you will be the slave of all." (Mark 10:42–44)

Then Jesus spoke to the crowds and to his disciples, saying, "The scribes and the Pharisees have taken their seat on the chair of Moses. Therefore, do and observe all things whatsoever they tell you, but do not follow their example. For they preach but they do not practice. They tie up heavy burdens [hard to carry] and lay them on people's shoulders, but they will not lift a finger to move them." (Matthew 23:1–4)

> Like a roaring lion or a ravenous bear
>   is a wicked ruler over a poor people.
>
>   (Proverbs 28:15)

> Should the anger of the ruler burst upon you, forsake not your place; for mildness abates great offenses.
>
>   (Ecclesiastes 10:4)

> Kindness and piety safeguard the king,
>   and he upholds his throne by justice.
>
>   (Proverbs 20:28)

> If a king is zealous for the rights of the poor,
>   his throne stands firm forever.
>
>   (Proverbs 29:14)

For we do not have a high priest who is unable to sympathize with our weaknesses, but one who has similarly been tested in every way, yet without sin. (Hebrews 4:15)

Church Documents

> It is an injustice and at the same time a grave evil and a disturbance of right order to transfer to the larger and higher collectivity functions which can be performed and provided for by the lesser and subordinate bodies. Inasmuch as every social activity should, by its very nature, prove a help to members of the body social, it should never destroy of absorb them.
>
>   (Pope Pius XI, *Quadragesimo Anno*, no. 79)

The *principle of subsidiarity* must be respected: "A community of a higher order should not interfere in the internal life of a community of a lower order, depriving the latter of its functions, but rather should support it in case of need and help to coordinate its activities with the activities of the rest of society, always with a view to the common good."[8]

(Pope John Paul II, *Centesimus Annus*, no. 48)

The primary norm for determining the scope and limits of governmental intervention is *"the principle of subsidiarity"* (*Centesimus Annus*, no. 48). This principle states that, in order to protect basic justice, government should undertake only those initiatives which exceed the capacities of individuals or private groups acting independently. Government should not replace or destroy smaller communities and individual initiative. Rather it should help them contribute more effectively to social well being and supplement their activity when the demands of justice exceed their capacities. This does not mean, however, that the government that governs least governs best. Rather it defines good government intervention as that which truly "helps" other social groups contribute to the common good by directing, urging, restraining, and regulating economic activity as "the occasion requires and necessity demands."[9]

(USCCB, *Economic Justice for All,* no. 124)

Lesson 9: Who Decides?

Learning Objectives

- The students will be able to describe how it feels when the principle of subsidiarity is not practiced.
- The students will learn the main reasons why people live in poverty by meeting a person who lives in poverty and asking questions of her or him.

The purpose of this activity is to allow the students to have some interaction with a person who is economically poor, and to understand the Church's teaching on subsidiarity. The students should learn the unique struggles of that person's life, and should compare the person's situation with their own contrasting stereotypes.

There are many stereotypes about those who are poor; unfortunately, many of them are negative (for example, they are lazy or drunk all the time). It is critical to this curriculum that students have a chance to meet with one or two people who are economically poor in order to break these stereotypes and personalize the issues around poverty, and to clarify the notion of poverty and the organizations that try to help. They should learn that people who are poor are often left out of decisions that affect their lives, and that they are "just like us," but with less money.

The students should meet the person who is economically poor at a social service agency. If the students live in a middle- or upper-class neighborhood, seeing a social service agency can be an eye-opening experience. Because this activity requires a trip to a social service agency, planning for this activity should take place well in advance.

The trip to the social service agency begins with the students having to solve a problem. The students will be divided into two groups. Both groups will be charged with coming up with a solution. After the two groups resolve the problem, the students then meet the agency's client. A person from the agency or the outside presenter will interview the client. Questions should be asked that elicit answers appropriate for young people to hear. Lunch or snacks will need to be provided by the outside presenter, the teacher, or the social service agency.

1. Pick the social service agency you and the outside presenter want the students to visit. The agency should be made aware of the *That's Not Fair* program and the guidelines for this lesson plan. The agency will need to provide a representative to work with you to set up the trip, select the client to meet with the students, provide the students with information about the agency, and provide two meeting rooms.

2. Prepare the participants. The teacher or outside presenter will need to meet with the agency's representative and the client. The lesson plan should be covered in depth so everyone is aware of the activity.

- Talk with the client about the boundaries of the conversation. The client should not be asked to "bare his or her soul" to the children. The interaction must be carried out with the utmost respect for the person sharing his or her story. The client should share stories that reflect his or her economic struggles and personal strengths. For example: "I can't afford to take my kids to the movies, so we come up with other forms of entertainment at home," or, "I can't buy new clothes for my kids, but thanks to my faith in God, we are still provided for." The general tone of the speaker should be upbeat and dignified. Overall, the dialogue should give the students an insight into the unique struggles of economic poverty.
- The outside presenter or a person from the social service agency should conduct the interview. Invite questions from the students afterward. If a question is asked that is too personal, the speaker needs to respectfully decline to answer. The students should be told ahead of time that any questions that are too personal will not be answered. Some students may not realize their questions are too personal.
- A representative from the agency should tell the students about the agency's services, give the students a tour, and provide a brief history of the agency (for example, why it was started, who funds the agency, any relevant stories the children may find interesting). Again, invite questions.

The Lesson

Instructions for the Outside Presenter

1. When the students arrive at the agency, they should be welcomed by the agency's representative and taken to the room where they will be eating lunch or a snack. In this example the students will have pizza. The room should have only about ten chairs, or less than half the number of students you have brought.

2. Tell the students that there are not enough chairs for all the students to sit down: "We have a problem. There are not enough chairs, so we need to figure out how we are going to eat pizza without enough chairs."

3. Divide the students into two groups: those students who were "rich" in the M&M's game and those who were "poor."

4. Take the "poor" students to another part of the building to problem solve. Have them sit on the floor for this discussion.

5. Allow the "rich" students to stay in the room and sit in the available chairs for their discussion.

6. An adult should lead the discussion with each group. The two discussions should take place simultaneously.

- *"Rich" group.* The conversation with the "rich" group should try to solicit solutions from them. They may say things like, "We can share the chairs," or, "Some of us can eat on the floor."

  After a few minutes, tell them that you know where there are more chairs and if they are all willing to set them up, there will be enough for all. Convince or tell them that this is the solution. Furthermore, tell them that because they are the more powerful group, they will mandate this decision to the others. No matter what solutions the other group may come up with, they are to stand firm and mandate this decision. Pick a group spokesperson, and tell the others to support the spokesperson should the other group challenge the decision.

- *"Poor" group.* The adult leading the "poor" group should listen to any ideas they may have. Then announce to the group a "great idea." Tell them that you have a blanket in your car and you could spread it out on the floor and have an "indoor picnic." Furthermore, you'll run out for some sodas and treats to have with the food. Sell the students on this idea to the point where they are excited about it.

7. The two groups will then reconvene in the larger room, whereupon the rich group will announce its solution. The "poor" group will try to make their solution known, but the "rich" group will not entertain it. The adult leader will then side with the "rich" group, and its decision will be enacted.

8. During lunch (or snack), tell the students that this exercise was planned. Ask them if they know what its message was. Listen for: "The people who are poor are not listened to." "We (those who are poor) had a good idea, but we never got a chance to say it." "The rich always get their way."

9. Ask the following questions:
- "How did it feel not to be listened to or not to have your idea implemented?"
- "Did it seem that rules were made for you to follow that you didn't find fair?"
- "Because you were poor, did it seem that you had no voice—no authority?"

10. Introduce the representative from the agency. The representative should talk about the services the agency provides, why and when the agency was founded, how the agency gets its funding, and so on.

11. Introduce the agency's client. The outside presenter or the agency's representative then conducts the interview. The client should be asked about a time when she or he did not feel listened to simply because she or he was poor. Prepare the client ahead of time for this question, and describe for them ahead of time the activity the students went through.

12. After the interview is over, allow the students to ask the client some questions. Allow the students to ask whatever they want to ask. If they, due to their youthfulness, ask a question that is too personal, for example, "Why don't you have a husband?" gently tell the student that this is a personal question and the client won't answer it. The students might ask things like, "What's some things your children would like but you cannot afford?"

Connect the activity and the visit with the low-income person to the concept of subsidiarity, that is, allowing people to make decisions for themselves. The agency's representative may give the students a tour of the agency before they go back to school.

UNIT FIVE

Understanding Charity

Theological Background: "Charity Cases"

A bearded elderly man came into our pantry at 4:15 p.m. with a little girl. I assumed them to be grandfather and granddaughter. He said to me, "I know by the sign on your door that your pantry closed fifteen minutes ago, but can we please have some food?" I said, "Yes, of course." Immediately he looked up and said, "Thank you, Lord."

That man and his granddaughter are just two of thousands of people who are poor that come to pantries sponsored by our parishes throughout the Kansas City metropolitan area.

A question that I, and I suspect, my peers, have been asked many times is, "Do you screen the people who come to you for food?" I think what is implied by that question is a statement, "I hope you give food just to those who really deserve it."

To give anything to someone because he or she deserves it is just. As a country, we pride ourselves on being just. According to Superman, along with truth, justice is the American way. The American way of justice can sometimes be construed as quite self-centered: giving to each person what is due, keeping what you earn, believing there's no such thing as a free lunch, and scratching another's back only if he scratches mine.

It is good to be just. However, the Gospels teach us to practice charity that exceeds justice: to give to people more than they deserve. If someone asks you to walk one mile, walk two; if they ask for your shirt, give them your coat as well. It's not really American to practice charity that exceeds justice . . . but it's quite Christian.

Every Christmas we celebrate this teaching. On that day all of us will be recipients of charity. All of us will get gifts from family and friends that we did not deserve. Parenthetically, I might add, if our family and friends really screened us, we probably wouldn't fare as well at Christmas.

It's not only at Christmas that we get things we don't deserve. When I think about my own life more deeply, I realize I have received lots of gifts I didn't earn. I didn't deserve the two caring parents that raised me. I didn't deserve my five supportive brothers and sisters. I didn't deserve the food on the table that my father brought home and my mother cooked. I didn't deserve the safe neighborhood I grew up in. I didn't deserve the educational opportunities provided for me.

Many of us probably received similar gifts early on in life. And because of those gifts, we are considered in the eyes of others, for the most part, "successful." We don't have to go to food pantries for food, and we don't live in shelters. However, our successes are an illusion. The illusion is that we have earned our successes. The reality is that we were all given gifts from above that we didn't deserve. We are all charity cases.

When I told the elderly man and his granddaughter that I would give them food, the man immediately looked upward and thanked God. You can say many things about that man, but you can't say he suffers from any illusions. At least he knows from where his food comes. At least he knows that everything in life is a gift from God. At least he knows that he is a charity case. I think this is why he will enter the Kingdom of God first.

Lesson 10: An Act of Charity

Learning Objectives

- The students will refresh their memories of the definitions of charity and justice.
- The students will work in groups to develop one act of charity they can carry out.

The purpose of this activity is to review the differences between charity and justice, and to come up with an act of charity that the class will complete.

1. Review what the students learned from the visit to the social service agency: "What did you learn at the agency? What did you think of (name of the client)? What are some of the things you remember about that person?"

2. Compare and contrast their answers to what they said at the beginning of the program about people who are poor: "Think back to the beginning of this program. You were asked, 'What picture do you see in your mind when you hear the term *poor person* (see lesson 2)?'" Then ask these questions:
- "Do you still see the same kind of person?"
- "What were some messages from the 'Who Decides?' activity in lesson 9?"

3. Review the difference between charity and justice: "Since the beginning of this program, we have talked about the difference between charity and justice. Tell me again what that difference is." [Charity is giving some specific item to a person who is in need, for example, a used coat. Justice is changing a law to help a large number of people who are poor.]

4. Begin a discussion on charity with these comments: "We will be working on an act of justice later in the program. But let's talk about charity now. Today I would like you to brainstorm within your group to come up with an idea for an act of charity that could help (the name of the client) or (the name of the social service agency)."

5. Allow time for brainstorming and discussion.

6. Ask each group to share its ideas, and write those ideas on the chalkboard.

7. Ask the class to come to an agreement on one act of charity the class can carry out.

8. Ask the students what steps need to be taken to carry out this act of charity. Write the steps on the chalkboard.

9. Ask the students to develop a time line for when they want this act of charity to be completed, and then carry out the plan. You may find that you need to enlist the help of volunteer parents to coordinate and carry out the class's plan.

UNIT SIX

Solidarity

Theological Background: "Am I My Brother's Keeper?"

I once traveled to San Diego with a friend to watch the Kansas City Chiefs play a football game against the Chargers. My friend and I did some sightseeing the day before the game. He wore his red Chiefs' jersey. Periodically he would be spotted by some other Chiefs' fans wearing red jerseys and was greeted with "Go, Chiefs!"

Though strangers, their Chiefs' jerseys gave them a bond.

Many things can bond people: blood, nationality, skin color, age, language, type of clothing, occupation, religion, interests, school. Given the right situation, it doesn't take much to feel "connected" to another person. Two Americans who meet unexpectedly in a foreign country might act like long lost friends. Meeting a stranger who attended the same high school as you did can advance the relationship immediately.

What has the ability to unite us also has the ability to divide us. While in San Diego for the game, my friend was spotted by someone wearing a Chargers' jersey, who then treated him to a mock taunting: "We're going to beat you tomorrow!"

The virtue of solidarity, as taught by the Church, is the ability to look past all the superficial things that can unite or divide us, and to see deeper. A deeper look at another person reveals that she or he was made by the same God who made me. Therefore we are bonded at the level of "being."

In a land that promotes self-sufficiency and wealth, those who are dependent and poor are often disparaged. The frequently spoken challenge to those who are poor, "Why don't you get a job?" is said with a tone of derision and not compassion. The person who is poor is seen as someone "other than me." Yet, the Catholic *Catechism* challenges us to see all people as "another self."

It's amazing how something as simple as a Chiefs' jersey can bond people. It is unfortunate that the deeper bond of God's love that unites us all is more difficult to see.

Bible Quotes

Then the LORD asked Cain, "Where is your brother Abel?" He answered, "I do not know. Am I my brother's keeper?" (Genesis 4:9)

"Which of these three, in your opinion, was neighbor to the robbers' victim?" He answered, "The one who treated him with mercy." Jesus said to him, "Go and do likewise." (Luke 10:36–37)

"I pray not only for them, but also for those who will believe in me through their word, so that they may all be one, as you, Father, are in me and I in you, that they also may be in us, that the world may believe that you sent me." (John 17:20–21)

As a body is one though it has many parts, and all the parts of the body, though many, are one body, so also Christ. (1 Corinthians 12:12)

"Then he will say to those on his left, 'Depart from me, you accursed, into the eternal fire prepared for the devil and his angels.'" (Matthew 25:41)

He said to him, "You shall love the Lord, your God, with all your heart, with all your soul, and with all your mind. This is the greatest and the first commandment. The second is like it: You shall love your neighbor as yourself." (Matthew 22:37–39)

> God created man in his image;
> in the divine image he created him;
> male and female he created them.
>
> (Genesis 1:27)

Church Documents

[Solidarity] is not a feeling of vague compassion or shallow distress at the misfortunes of so many people, both near and far. On the contrary, it is a firm and persevering determination to commit oneself to the common good; that is to say, to the good of all and of each individual, because we are all really responsible for all.
(Pope John Paul II, *Sollicitudo Rei Socialis,* no. 38)

We have to move from our devotion to independence, through an understanding of interdependence, to a commitment to human solidarity. That challenge must find its realization in the kind of community we build among us. Love implies concern for all—especially people who are poor—and a continued search for those social and economic structures that permit everyone to share in a community that is a part of a redeemed creation. (Romans 8:21–23)
(USCCB, *Economic Justice for All,* p. 365)

We have inherited from past generations, and we have benefited from the work of our contemporaries: for this reason we have obligations toward all, and we cannot refuse to interest ourselves in those who will come after us to enlarge the human family. The reality of human solidarity, which is a benefit for us, also imposes a duty.

(Pope Paul VI, *Populorum Progressio*, no. 17)

Yet, today men are so intimately associated in all parts of the world that they feel, as it were, as if they are members of one and the same household. Therefore, the nations that enjoy a sufficiency and abundance of everything may not overlook the plight of other nations whose citizens experience such domestic problems that they are all but overcome by poverty and hunger, and are not able to enjoy basic human rights.

(Pope John XXIII, *Mater et Magistra*, no. 157)

Solidarity is an undoubtedly Christian virtue. In the light of faith, solidarity seeks to go beyond itself, to take on the specifically Christian dimension of total gratuity, forgiveness, and reconciliation.

(Pope John Paul II, *Sollicitudo Rei Socialis*, no. 40)

Solidarity helps us to see the "other"—whether a person, people, or nation—not just as some kind of instrument, with a work capacity and physical strength to be exploited at low cost and then discarded when no longer useful, but as our "neighbor," a "helper" (cf. Gn 2:18–20), to be made a sharer, on a par with ourselves in the banquet of life to which all are equally invited by God.

(Pope John Paul II, *Sollicitudo Rei Socialis*, no. 39)

Lesson 11: Loop Game

Learning Objective

- Students will engage in an activity to help them appreciate what solidarity is and what it means to practice Christian solidarity.

The purpose of this activity is to understand that we are all connected. This lesson requires some advance work. You will need one fabric loop for each student. The loop can be made of pieces of yarn or strips of fabric. Each loop should be about two or three feet in diameter.

1. Have the students form a single line, shoulder to shoulder, at one end of the gym.

2. Instruct each student to step into a loop and pull it up to his or her waist.

3. Now have each student take his or her right hand and grab the loop of the person on his or her right. Do the same with the left hand. Each loop will have two hands on it: one from the person on the right, and one from the person on the left.

4. Explain to the students that they are to see how quickly they can get to the other end of the gym. However, they must follow these rules:
- Stay connected.
- Move as quickly as possible.
- No one is to get hurt.

5. "Ready, set, go!" The first trial should go quickly and smoothly.

6. Now get ready to do it a second time. Secretly inform two students near one end of the line that on the word "go," they are to hop on one foot, and that they can release their hands on the loops if necessary to avoid getting hurt.

7. "Ready, set, go!" During the second trial, the "hoppers" will have a difficult time keeping up and may fall at some point. The rest of the line will continue forward.

8. After the second trial, remind the students that the rules state that no one is to get hurt and everyone is to stay connected. Ask them what went wrong.

9. Now get ready to do it a third time. Tell the students, "We are going to try this again."

10. "Ready, set, go!"

11. Here's what should have happened: the first time the students ran to the other side of the gym, they all stayed connected and, for the most part, they ran together; that is, it should have looked like a long, straight line running down the gym floor.

On the second and third attempts, because two students had to hop on one leg, the line of running students will not be so straight; rather, it will have a noticeable "dip" in it. The students who are farthest away from the hopping students probably will not even notice the dip. This is important for the discussion later. Possibly the students who are hopping may fall and become disconnected from the group. Again, if this happens this is important to talk about in the discussion.

Return to the classroom to discuss the game. (It is best to have the discussion in the classroom, as it sends the message that the "playful" game is over; now is the time for learning.) Ask questions such as these:
- "What was the message you got out of this activity?"
- "Did anyone notice how the shape of the line from the first run differed from the shape of the line in the second and third runs?" You might call on someone who does *not* raise their hand. They may not have noticed the difference. If they did not, ask them where they were in the line. Odds are they were not near the "dip." Then

call on someone who did notice the difference and ask them to explain it.

Share with the students, "Often we are so busy in life that we do not even notice those who are falling behind. Or we may notice them, but the pull of the whole line is so strong, it makes it difficult to slow down and help those who are falling behind. This is the reality between the 'haves' and the 'have-nots.' Most people are not cold-hearted about helping people who are poor; rather, they are just too blind or too busy. Once they are exposed to the needs of others, the 'haves' are willing to help."

The discussion ought to continue with a particular focus on economic poverty. Continue with these questions:

- "Who do you think the hoppers represented?" [Answer: people who are poor.]
- "What do the loops represent?" [Answer: Because God created all of us, we are connected.]
- "What do you suppose this parable is trying to teach us?" [Answer: We need to pay attention to any of our brothers and sisters who are falling behind.]

You might bring it into their work by asking, "In this school, do students stay connected or do we disconnect ourselves from certain people?" Listen for responses such as these:

- "The rich move on in life while neglecting the hurting people who are poor."
- "Some people cannot get through life as easily as others."
- "Rich people should slow down and help a person who is poor when she or he is struggling and needs a little help."

12. Discuss how solidarity means working together for each other. John Paul II says that solidarity is a virtue that when practiced, means that we see all others as truly our neighbors.

UNIT SEVEN

Understanding Social Structures

Theological Background: "Ropes that Bind"

I read a story somewhere about a man in India who owned an elephant. To prevent the elephant from roaming around, he tied its back leg with a rope and then anchored the rope with a relatively small peg. Someone asked the man how this simple rope and peg could restrain the large elephant. Surely, if the elephant wanted to, it could simply take a step and be immediately free.

The man replied that he'd had this elephant since it was born. From the earliest days, he had used this simple restraint when the elephant was small and physically unable to break loose. He said that now the elephant simply does not know it is strong enough to break free. The elephant assumes there is nothing it can do about the rope, so it does not even try to pull free.

All of us grew up with "ropes" attached to us.

"Ropes" refer to any rules or structures that hold us in place. Some are good. One rope my parents attached to my siblings and me while we were young was that we had to read for one hour a day. That was a good rope. To this day my siblings and I all like to read.

Some ropes are bad. Prior to the 1960s, blacks in certain parts of our country could not eat in the same restaurants as whites.

Rules and social structures become such a part of our daily living that, like the grown elephant, we don't even realize that we are "tied up."

Jesus healed a man on the Sabbath. Jewish law required that no work be done on the Sabbath—not even healing. Jesus questioned and broke the literal understanding of that rule. The value of helping a person in need was greater than strict adherence to a rule.

Like Jesus, our Church encourages us to question rules or structures, and if we find them to be harmful or sinful, we should try to change them. Pope John Paul II considers any rule a "structure of sin" when it gets in the way of peace and the development of a human person.

We are more accustomed to talking about sins as "actions" rather than "structures." It is easy to see sinful actions. A man robs a bank. A student cheats on a test. A child lies to her mother. It is more difficult to see sinful structures. A tax law burdens people who are poor. A housing policy discriminates against people of color. A Medicaid statute does not pay for some prescription medicines.

Seeing societal structures, judging them according to the values of our faith, and then acting on our faith to make sure all structures are fair is what justice is all about. It's how the elephant is set free.

Bible Quotes

He said to them, "Which one of you who has a sheep that falls into a pit on the sabbath will not take hold of it and lift it out? How much more valuable a person is than a sheep. So it is lawful to do good on the sabbath." (Matthew 12:11–12)

Then he said to them, "Is it lawful to do good on the sabbath rather than to do evil, to save life rather than to destroy it?" But they remained silent. (Mark 3:4)

And he said, "Woe also to you scholars of the law! You impose on people burdens hard to carry, but you yourselves do not lift one finger to touch them." (Luke 11:46)

Bear one another's burdens, and so you will fulfill the law of Christ. (Galatians 6:2)

Then Peter said to her, "Why did you agree to test the Spirit of the Lord? Listen, the footsteps of those who have buried your husband are at the door, and they will carry you out." (Acts 5:9)

There is but one rule for you and for the resident alien, a perpetual rule for all your descendants. Before the LORD you and the alien are alike. (Numbers 15:15)

Church Documents

Rulers should anxiously safeguard the community and all its parts . . . the safety of the commonwealth is not only the first law but is a government's whole reason of existence.
> (Pope Leo XIII, *Rerum Novarum,* no. 28)

Economic life must be inspired by Christian principles.
> (Pope Pius XI, *Quadragesimo Anno,* no. 136)

One may not take as the ultimate criteria in economic life the interests of individuals or organized groups, nor unregulated competition, nor excessive power on the part of the wealthy, nor the vain honor of the nation or its desire for domination, nor anything of this sort. Rather it is necessary that economic undertakings be governed by justice and charity as the principle law of social life.
> (Pope John XXIII, *Mater et Magistra,* no. 38)

The order which prevails in society is by nature moral. Grounded as it is in truth, it must function according to the norms of justice, it should be inspired and perfected by mutual love, and finally it should be brought to an ever more refined and human balance in freedom.

(Pope John XXIII, *Pacem in Terris*, no. 37)

The church considers it her duty to speak out on work from the viewpoint of its human value and of the moral order to which it belongs, and she sees this as one of her important tasks within the service that she renders to the evangelical message as a whole.

(Pope John Paul II, *Laborem Exercens*, no. 24)

One must denounce the existence of economic, financial, and social mechanisms which, although they are manipulated by people, often function almost automatically, thus accentuating the situation of wealth for some and poverty for the rest.

(Pope John Paul II, *Sollicitudo Rei Socialis*, no. 16)

Lesson 12: Jumping Through Ropes

Instructions for the Outside Presenter

1. Ask the students to sit in a square. There should be a foot of space between each of them.

2. Ask the students to give you some of the rules they are expected to follow while in school, for example: "No running in the halls." "School begins at 8:00 a.m." "Thirty minutes for recess." "You must wear a school uniform."

After the students call out just one or two rules, encourage them to name rules they don't like, for example: "No tackle football." "No soda pop at lunch." "Shirts must always be tucked in."

The message of this activity is more easily made when the students voice school rules they feel are unfair. The students will more easily relate to people who are poor, who feel there are unfair societal rules.

3. Whenever a student calls out a rule, hand her or him one end of the clothesline rope, and stretch the rope to the student sitting across from her or him on the other side of the square. Cut the rope.

4. The teacher should write down the rules the students are citing. Hopefully, one student from each side of the square will call out a rule. Ask: "How about someone on this side of the square? What is a rule you are expected to follow?"

5. When at least one student from each side of the square has cited a rule, you will have created a "rope web." Have the students pull on the rope and then lay it neatly on the ground.

6. Leave the rope on the ground and ask all the students to stand up.

7. Divide them into two groups: the "rich" ones from the M&M's game form one group and the "poor" ones from the M&M's game form the other group. Have the rich group line up single file by a corner of the rope web.

8. Tell them you are going to have a game to see which group can walk through the web the fastest without coming in contact with the rope. But there are rules to this exercise:

- Each student must step (with one foot only) in each of the squares created by the rope.
- If they touch the rope, there is a 10-second penalty.

9. Have the first group go. Time them.

10. When the first group is finished, tell the second group to get ready. However, before they begin, tell the first group to sit back down around the perimeter of the web and grab all the ends of the rope. Each student will probably need to grab an end in each hand. Tell them to lift the rope web about a foot off the ground.

11. Now tell the second group to walk through. The second group will be larger, so use the same number of students as were in the first group. Time them. Obviously the second group will have more trouble. They will have to go slower, will touch the rope, and may even fall. Once again, the poor group loses.

12. When the second group is done, you might give candy bars to the winners. (Though the giving of prizes is optional, it does add a visceral learning to the game. The winners feel rewarded, and the losers feel slighted.)

13. Return to the classroom to discuss the game. (It is best to have the discussion in the classroom, as it sends the message that the "playful" game is over; now is the time for learning.)

14. Initiate a discussion with this question: "What was the purpose of this game?" Listen for: "Some rules make it tougher on people who are poor." "The ropes represent rules." "Those holding the ropes are those who are in power." "Some rules are good; some are bad." "Those in power can walk around rules more easily."

15. Talk about the school's rules: "Why do the teachers have different rules than the students?" For example, teachers may have soda pop every day for lunch if they want. Have the students name some of the rules of the school. Have the students identify rules that seem unfair to them or rules that apply only to some and not others.

16. Using the metaphor of the rope web, ask the following questions:
- "Who can change rules?" [Answer: Those holding the ropes.]
- "How can people who are poor change the rules?" [Answer: By expressing their desires to the rule makers.]

17. For a homework assignment, provide each student with handout 8, a list of the school rules that were mentioned during the game. Ask them to choose three rules and write out whether they believe each rule is fair or not fair and why.

HOMEWORK

Directions

Choose three of the rules we talked about today. Check whether you think the rule is fair or unfair and explain why.

Fair   Unfair

— — We can't chew gum.

— — We can't play tackle football.

— — We can't run in the building.

— — We must not talk during fire drills.

— — Socks must be able to be seen above shoes.

— — Pop is allowed only at lunch on Thursdays.

— — Sweatshirts may not be tied.

— — Teachers may drink pop in the classroom.

Lesson 13: Challenging Rules Appropriately

In preparation for this lesson, you will want to spend time with the principal of your school to discuss the purpose of the lesson and agree on the content of it. This is important so that you and the principal have a shared understanding of what will happen in the classroom with the students, and so the principal is not caught off-guard, blind-sided by the students' questions. Because the topic is discussion of student perceptions on the fairness of school rules, it is important to be clear about who really does have the authority to change rules within the school. The principal may not have the authority. Rather, it may be a school board or a pastor or group of pastors, or it may be a diocesan rule that is mandated by the Office of the Bishop. You'll want to make sure that the scope of the discussion in this program is limited to those rules that are within the bounds of being open for discussion.

1. Direct the students to have on their desks the homework from the previous class.

2. Tell the students that their principal will be coming to their class to talk about school rules. Quickly review how to question the principal respectfully.

3. When the principal arrives, explain, in front of the class, that the students are learning about fair and unfair rules in society, and part of this activity is looking at the rules they have to follow.

4. Suggest to the students that if they make a successful challenge to the principal, he or she ought to change the rule. Have the principal agree to this suggestion.
(In one school the students questioned a rule that said that after taking off their sweatshirts, they could not tie the arms of their school sweatshirts around their waist because it was too casual. The students challenged the principal that on some days, the temperature started out cool and then warmed up. They didn't wear their sweatshirts this way to "dress down" but rather as a matter of convenience and comfort. The principal agreed with them and changed the rule.)

5. Introduce the first rule, and ask the students to share with the principal their thoughts on why they think the rule is fair or unfair. The principal should respond to the thoughts of the students and help the students understand the reasoning of the school for the particular rule under discussion. Ask the students if after hearing the explanation about the reason for the rule, their perception has changed at all.

6. After the discussion of each rule with the principal, ask the principal if she or he was troubled by any of the perceptions of the

students. Ask the students to describe how they felt listened to by the principal.

7. Tell the students that this was a respectful way to discuss an issue with a person in authority.

This exercise helps to lay the groundwork for questioning elected officials later in the course. The students are very aware of their school rules. They may feel some are unfair, and they know there are reasons why rule makers and people in authority have the responsibility to see to it that rules are followed. Next they will study the laws of society. Making the transition from school rules to society laws will be much easier now.

UNIT EIGHT

The Issue

Action for Justice

The previous lessons have laid the theological groundwork for what is ahead. Your students have learned the difference between charity and justice, and why we are called by our Church to work on issues of justice. In the next few weeks, your students will work on an issue of justice on behalf of those in need.

A social justice issue will need to be chosen for the students to work on. Choosing a particular social justice issue for the students to work on can be a difficult and time-consuming task. You may want to have a team of teachers in your school work together to identify some options for the students to consider. Another option, to assist you, is to consult with someone at the diocesan social justice office or someone in leadership with Catholic Charities.

At the point in the lesson where the students have the chosen social justice issue explained to them so that they fully understand it, you may wish to bring in an outside expert on the issue. After they understand the issue, they will prepare for two presentations by writing a script and making posters that illustrate the issue. The students will use these posters when making their first presentation to their parish to enlist community support. Finally, they will meet with one or more government officials to lobby on behalf of those in need.

After a social justice issue is chosen for the students to work on, you will need to determine who is a decision maker involved with the social justice issue. Is the decision maker a city council member? your city's mayor? or a state senator or representative? You may have more than one decision maker. You will need to start contacting this person to set up a time for the students to meet with him or her. These steps are described in more detail on the following pages.

Choosing an Issue

Here are some general principles to follow when choosing a social justice issue:

- Choose an issue that is relevant to the local community. Admittedly there are injustices around the globe, but to best connect with the students, choose something that's under your nose. Some examples include low-income housing in your city, a state earned-income tax credit, or improving foster care in your state. If you did pick an international issue, connect it locally. Let's say the issue you want to address is the injustice of child labor in Indonesia.

See if a local department store buys from companies that sanction this practice. Then talk to a representative from the local department store.

- Choose an issue the students can understand. The death penalty is probably easier to grasp than an issue involving international trade agreements. I have found that choosing an issue that affects children their own age works best, for example, improving foster care in the state. Another school worked on improving conditions for children in homeless shelters.

- Choose an issue that educates. Some issues are too complex or even too controversial for sixth graders to handle. For example, the pros and cons of capitalism versus socialism are inappropriate at this level.

- Choose an issue that is connected to the lessons in this program. Whatever issue you select, make sure you can tie it to the lessons you have taught. Otherwise this program will be more of a civics class than a class on Catholic social teaching. Always remember that all issues are related to the Church's understanding of human dignity. An issue like improving the sidewalks and curbs near your school, though needed, misses the depth of Catholic social teaching. We've got bigger fish to fry than fixing some curbs.

- Choose an issue that is justice oriented. A justice-oriented issue relates to structures, laws, policies, or systems, and, if changed, will affect large numbers of people. A charity-oriented issue is usually a direct response to an individual or a small number of people. For example, collecting food for a pantry would be charity; trying to change a law to give tax rebates to working families that are poor would be justice.

Who Chooses the Issue?

After careful consideration and with appropriate input from others, you will need to have identified a social justice issue for the students to work on.

As an alternative, you could consider bringing to the students two issues that are possible for them to work on and allow them to choose the one they most prefer.

As noted in the introduction to this lesson, because of the complexity of the task of choosing a social justice issue to address as a class, it is best that adults with the proper training, experience, and knowledge identify an issue or issues for the class to work on.

After the issue has been chosen, the teacher should take two or three class sessions to fully explain the issue to the students. Alternatively, you may wish to bring in an expert on the issue to provide input to the students for these sessions, or a variety of experts who can present on the different aspects of the issue. A general description of the sessions for this exercise is provided in lesson 14 below.

You may choose to give a verbal quiz or test to ensure the students fully understand the issue. Take whatever time is needed until the students fully grasp the issue.

Finding an Issue

Choose an issue that has the support or advocacy of the Church, for example, your diocesan peace and justice office, your state Catholic Conference, or the United States Conference of Catholic Bishops. The people in these offices can help you identify an issue appropriate for your class. Be sure not to choose an issue on your own—you risk being accused of using the students for your own personal agenda, rather than the Church's agenda.

Find a Target for Advocacy

As you choose an issue, consider who will be the appropriate target for the class advocacy effort. Is your issue local? city, county, or state? national? Does it involve government, business, or some type of agency? Make sure to choose a target that has a say in the issue and wields some power to make a change.

Your target person should be someone with whom the students can meet. If the target person is a U.S. senator or representative, have the government official visit your school when she or he is in your city. If the target person is one of your state senators or representatives, then your students should travel to your state capitol or invite the government official to visit your school. If you elect to have the target person visit your school, you can do one of two things: have a general meeting in which the person visits your classroom or have a rally. Having a rally works best if other schools in your diocese work together on the same social justice issue.

Lesson 14: Explaining the Justice Issue

Learning Objectives

- Students will be able to articulate in their own words the chosen social justice issue that affects people living in poverty.
- Students will describe practical things that can be done to change the issue, so that those who live in poverty can live a "decent life."

Based on the social justice issue your class will be working on, talk with the outside presenter about developing an activity for your students. Your goal should be for the students to experience firsthand how the issue would affect them if they were someone who would benefit from their activism.

Sample Activity

Here is a description of how one teacher explained the meaning of an earned-income tax credit. In addition to understanding the issue, the teacher wanted the students to realize what part of their government is involved in the issue (and to whom the students would later make a presentation).

The issue chosen was a bill considering an earned-income tax credit for working families that was to be voted on in the Missouri state legislature. The Missouri Catholic Conference, an organization that monitors bills and their relationship to Church teaching, suggested the issue.

The students were each given a card with a role to play in an exercise. The exercise was designed to help them understand what the earned-income tax credit is. The various roles in the activity included being high-income family members, low-income family members, church parishioners, school students, a U.S. senator, a state senator, a city council person, and God.

Five students were part of a high-income family and were placed in one corner of the room. They were given a bowl containing two hundred beans. Another five students were part of a low-income family. They were placed in another corner of the room and given a bowl containing twenty beans. Those students representing elected officials stood in the front of the room. Those students representing the Church sat in a corner of the room. Those representing school students sat in the remaining corner. The student who represented God stood in the front of the room.

The teacher gave a brief description of taxes, and then explained how different percentages of taxes are paid to federal, state, and local governments, depending on a person's income. The "families" had to bring up the appropriate number of beans to put in the hands of the "elected officials" in the front of the room.

The students in the "low-income family" saw how quickly their beans were going and how few they had left. Though the students in the "high-income family" had to pay more beans in taxes, they were left with many more beans on which to live.

The teacher explained that the federal government has already decided to give an earned-income tax credit to working low-income families. That is, for those parents who are employed but do not earn enough, a "bean" was given back. The state government was considering following suit by giving a second "bean" back to each of the qualifying families.

After some discussion the teacher determined that the students understood the issue and that they would be talking to state government officials during their presentation.

They were then asked why they would want to speak on behalf of low-income working families. Based on what they learned in the previous lessons, the students pointed to the student standing on the desk and answered, "Because God created everyone and wants all of us to have a decent life." They further saw that God's voice on earth was the Church, that in this case God's voice was their parish, and that as students in the parish school, they were the voice of the parish.

By acting out all of this, the students were able to visualize more clearly what the trip to the state capitol was all about.

To convey this message to the parish, they spoke at all the Masses one Sunday and collected signature cards from the adults in support of the bill. The students later presented the signature cards to their state senators and representatives.

8

UNIT NINE

Vision

Theological Background: "Do you see what I see?"

There are two kinds of airplane pilots: those who can fly only when the sky is clear, and those who can fly in cloudy weather by using the airplane instruments. To be instrument rated, a person must undergo many more hours of training. These pilots are essentially trained to "see without seeing." Even in a dense cloud, these pilots, by virtue of modern technology and trusting their instruments, can fly their plane as if it were a clear day.

One reason why some American Catholics don't "take" to acts of justice is that it is hard to "see" what justice looks like. For some people visual images are less challenging to understand than mental images. Justice is an abstract matter and, therefore, can sometimes be hard to "see."

Charity can sometimes be easier to see than justice. Imagine asking the people in your parish to volunteer for Habitat for Humanity or the Justice Committee. When volunteering for Habitat, you can probably see yourself working on a house. When volunteering for the Justice Committee, you cannot "see" what you will be doing.

Like a pilot who is instrument rated, doing justice requires more training. One must be able to see the structures, rules, and systems that oppress people in order to do justice. They are difficult to see, but they are there.

Bible Quotes

> Without prophecy the people become demoralized;
>> but happy is he who keeps the law.
>
> (Proverbs 29:18)

Lies these prophets utter in my name, the LORD said to me. I did not send them; I gave them no command nor did I speak to them. Lying visions, foolish divination, dreams of their own imagination, they prophesy to you. (Jeremiah 14:14)

> Thus says the LORD of hosts:
> Listen not to the words of your prophets,
>> who fill you with emptiness;

Visions of their own fancy they speak,
    not from the mouth of the LORD.

(Jeremiah 23:16)

Sunk into the ground are her gates;
    he has removed and broken her bars.
Her king and her princes are among the pagans;
    priestly instruction is wanting,
and her prophets have not received
    any vision from the Lord.

(Lamentations 2:9)

Then the LORD answered me and said:
    Write down the vision
Clearly upon the tablets,
    so that one can read it readily.

(Habakkuk 2:2)

Son of man, you live in the midst of a rebellious house; they have eyes to see but do not see, and ears to hear but do not hear, for they are a rebellious house. (Ezekiel 12:2)

Church Documents

"For he who is, as it were, *a light in the Lord*, and walks as a *son of light*, perceives more clearly what the requirements of justice are." (Pope John XXIII, *Mater et Magistra,* no. 257)

"The Church has always had the duty of scrutinizing the signs of the times and interpreting them in the light of the Gospel." (Pope Paul VI *Gaudium et Spes,* no. 4)

"It belongs to the laymen, without waiting passively for orders and directives, to take the initiative freely and to infuse a Christian spirit into the mentality, customs, laws, and structures of the community in which they live." (Pope Paul VI, *Populorum Progressio,* no. 81)

Lesson 15: Illustrating the Issue

Learning Objectives

- Students will be able to articulate in their own words the chosen ties completed in the course to date.
- The students will illustrate the Church's teachings on social justice as it relates to the social justice issue they are working to address.

The purpose of this activity is for the students to prepare for a presentation to their parish on their chosen social justice issue. The students will review what they have learned, describe the social justice issue on which they are working, and prepare posters for use during their presentation.

Preparation

1. This activity may take up to two class periods to complete.

2. Prepare for the lesson. You will need an overhead projector or a chalkboard/marker board, drawing paper, poster board, and pencils.

3. Before the lesson, look over the examples on the following pages so that you have a clear idea of what is expected of the students. Your students will need to illustrate the chosen social justice issue in a series of pictures (imagine a slide show using posters instead of slides). If your students show these pictures to someone, he or she should be able to understand the issue. Review the lesson plan.

Lesson

1. Begin the lesson by reviewing what the students have learned so far. Ask them specific questions about the meanings of each game, the difference between charity and justice, and the challenges faced by those who live in poverty.
- M&M's game—charity and justice
- In God's Image—God creates us all, human dignity
- The Cost of a Decent Life—what it takes to live a decent life, why people live in poverty
- Who Decides?—breaking poverty stereotypes, unfair rules
- An Act of Charity—charity and justice, doing an act of charity
- Loop Game—solidarity, we are all connected
- Jumping Through Ropes—rules and their fairness

2. You will need to come up with ten to twelve statements that help summarize the basic messages of the different activities and how they apply to the issue you will be working on. Help the students put these statements into a logical sequence that begins with some of the key teachings of the Church and ends with asking for support on a particular issue (for example: God made everyone equal. God wants everyone to live a decent life. Some hard-working people can't live a decent life).

Make notes of these statements. They will be used in this lesson when the students start working on the illustrations for their presentation.

3. As you elicit statements from the students, record them on the overhead projector, chalkboard, or marker board. The statements should be sequential, starting with the basic messages about the Church's teachings and leading to their action for justice.

4. Tell the students that they are going to describe the chosen social justice issue through a series of black-and-white pictures. Brainstorm with the class for ideas of ways to illustrate the statements. The illustrations should be simple, with not much detail, so that they can be easily seen and understood by an audience.

5. Assign two or three students to each statement.

6. Have the students sketch the illustrations on drawing paper. Stress simplicity!

7. When everyone is satisfied that the drawings illustrate the statements, have the students use pencils to enlarge their drawings onto poster board.

8. Outline finished drawings with black marker so that they will be clearly visible to people at a distance

9. Type the statements so that they can be easily read during the presentation to the parish. (See a sample on the following pages.)

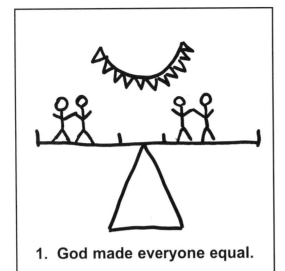

1. God made everyone equal.

2. God wants everyone to live a decent life.

3. Some hard-working people can't ive a decent life.

4. How can we change that?

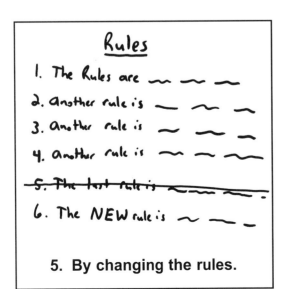

5. By changing the rules.

6. Everyone that works gets paid.

7. Everyone that works pays taxes.

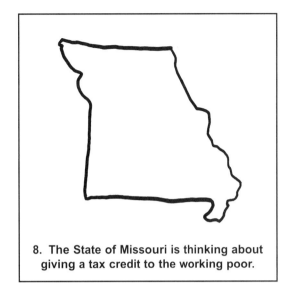

8. The State of Missouri is thinking about giving a tax credit to the working poor.

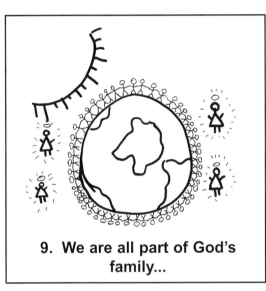

9. We are all part of God's family...

10. ...and some of our brothers and sisters need your help?

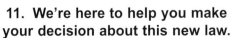

11. We're here to help you make your decision about this new law.

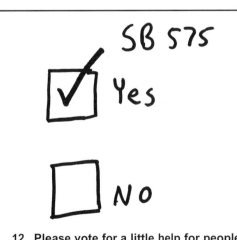

12. Please vote for a little help for people who are working hard and still having a tough time.

UNIT TEN

Presentation to the Parish

Lesson 16: Presentation to the Parish

As with any class presentation or performance, rehearsals are necessary. One class period should be sufficient for a rehearsal. The rehearsal should be completed a day or two before the presentation.

1. Involve each student in the presentation. There can be a number of roles to play, such as reader, prayer leader, greeter, poster board holder, and gatherers of signatures after Mass.

2. Choose readers that articulate well and can be heard when using a microphone.

3. Practice going through the poster presentation, keeping in mind that the students holding the posters will have to be positioned so that the audience has a good view.

Now your students should be ready for their presentation to the parish. After their presentation, save the posters. They can be used again when your students meet with an elected official (in the next lesson).

Spreading the WORD!

Advocating on behalf of people in need will be more successful if more people know about the issue. Here are some ideas for involving the parish and the community in your social justice issue:

- Use the parish bulletin or school newsletter. Beginning with the Sunday on which the students give their presentation, print regular updates about what the class is learning, what the justice issue involves, and how the students are following the call of the Gospels and Catholic social teaching.
- Let parishioners lend support. When the students give the presentation to the parish, offer postcards, letters, or petitions people can sign to show support of the issue. Save the signatures, as you will need them when the students meet with elected officials. Have several petition forms available should some adults wish to take them and get them signed by others.
- Work with the parish social justice committee. This group of people can be a great resource. They are often people with an understanding of and a passion for Catholic social teaching and social justice issues. Committee members may have leads on local issues and be willing to help with research. The committee might also have ways to spread the word about the class project and connec-

10

tions in the community to make advocacy easier. If your parish social justice committee is not currently working on local issues, encourage them to do so by working with you. If your parish does not have a social justice committee, now is the time to get one started.

Learning Objectives

- The students will gather adult support of the social justice issue by making a presentation to the parish.
- The students will gain experience speaking in public on behalf of those who are in need.

In this activity the students will make a presentation to the parish about their social justice issue. The presentation should be made at all the weekend Masses. Work with your pastor to schedule a presentation at the weekend Masses or at a special meeting. Sunday Mass is the ideal place. Work with your pastor or parish liturgy coordinator to determine the best place within, before, or after Mass for the student presentation.

You will need to work with your pastor to determine how he would like the students to give their presentation. You may want to encourage the pastor to take an active role in the presentation by giving the parish an overview of what the students have been learning. Remember, most adults are just as unfamiliar with Catholic social teaching as the children. Now is the perfect time to give the adults in your parish a brief lesson.

During the presentation the students will use the posters they made in the previous lesson, holding them up one at a time while another student reads the message. Picture this as a slide show with posters instead of slides. At the conclusion of the poster presentation, the students should appeal to the adults in the parish to support them in their cause by taking a specific action. The specific action depends on the social justice issue on which they are working. If your students will be meeting with elected officials, the specific action could be signing a letter addressed to the elected officials urging the officials to take the right action.

UNIT ELEVEN

Interacting with Government

What He or She Intends to Do About the Issue

Remember, the students are there to gain the support of the person for the social justice issue. That's what advocacy and lobbying is all about.

You will be setting up and meeting with your target legislator or a government or business leader.

Lesson 17: Meeting Legislators and Government or Business Leaders

Making Contact

Send the elected official or government or business leader an introductory letter by postal mail, fax, or e-mail explaining the program, the social justice issue the class is addressing, and a request to meet. A follow-up phone call is often necessary to keep the ball rolling. It may take two or three weeks to get an appointment scheduled. Planning ahead and offering a flexible schedule will help you get on the person's calendar. In your introductory letter and follow-up calls, make it as clear as possible that the students will be making a presentation to the elected official or government or business leader. Once a meeting is set, send a confirmation letter.

If you are traveling to an office, as opposed to hosting a guest, include the details of your travel plans. Schedule changes on the part of the elected official or government or business leader can be discouraging, but are a reality of political life. Try to be accepting of change, but don't hesitate to push for a renewed commitment. By including the travel plans in your confirmation letter, the elected official or government or business leader should become aware of what is involved in arranging the trip and hopefully will avoid making any last-minute changes that are not absolutely necessary.

If you plan on meeting with an elected official, keep in mind that the higher the level of government you try to access, the harder it can be to schedule an appointment. If you choose to meet with U.S. senators or representatives, be prepared to accept a meeting with a staff person instead. At that level of government, staff members handle many of the issues for elected officials. Meeting with the staff person can be beneficial to your cause and just as much of an educational experience.

Getting Ready

The meeting with the government official is an action for justice. During the meeting, the students should present their understanding of the social justice issue and the reason why they think it ought to be changed. They should be explicit about their religious motivations.

Assign roles and speaking parts. Be sure the students know their roles and are comfortable with the speaking parts. The students need to be organized and respectful. An organized and disciplined group is a sign of power, and the group's message will have a better chance of being heard.

It would be appropriate for the students to begin the visit with a prayer. Role-playing and rehearsing their visit a number of times in advance would be helpful.

The official the students meet with should be briefed ahead of time so that neither side is blind-sided or surprised. This briefing leads to a more fruitful dialogue.

The students need to be clear about what they want from the meeting, whether it's a commitment to make a change or a clear explanation why a change will not be made. When appropriate, the students should present the signatures from the adults in their parish to show support of their cause and the social justice issue.

Consider what you will do following the presentation. Usually it is good to let the elected official respond to the students' message. Following that, you may want to have students ready with follow-up questions. Encourage the students to come up with their own questions. Get these ahead of time. Following are some examples:

- Do you agree with our position? If not, why? What can be done to change your mind? (You will want to prepare the students for negative news.)
- What will you do to help this cause?
- What did you think of our presentation?

Alert the Media

Media coverage is a good way to spread the word and it is fun for young people to see themselves in the paper or on television. Plus, the local news has plenty of stories about the bad things that happen in communities. Here's a chance for reporters to cover something positive: young people involved in faith and citizenship. When preparing for the advocacy presentation to elected officials, consider contacting your city newspaper, diocesan newspaper, and local television or radio stations to cover the event. If you are unsure about taking the first step, call your diocesan public relations office and see if they have a public relations representative who can help you get started. Or call the diocesan newspaper and ask for suggestions.

Lesson 18: Visiting the State Capitol

There are three ways your students can present their "poor man's PowerPoint" presentation to legislators: (1) at the capitol or another government building, (2) in your classroom, or (3) in a gymnasium or large auditorium if you have several other diocesan schools taking part in this program.

The purpose of this activity is to present the Church's values and the needs of people who are poor or marginalized to political or commercial leaders. This is at the heart of what the Church understands by doing justice; that is, influencing the laws and structures of our society with our values.

Advocacy at the state capitol can be an incredible experience. It also can be a lot more work for you than arranging a meeting at the school. Before scheduling your trip to your state capitol, check to confirm that the legislature is in session during the time you wish to visit. You want the elected officials to be there when you visit! Schedules vary from state to state. Remember to meet with both your senators and your representatives. (If you are concerned about the amount of work a trip will take, consider enlisting help from some of the students' parents.)

There are two ways to approach a meeting with legislators. One way is to call and set up appointments for the day of the visit. The other way is to arrive without a scheduled appointment. If you are unable to schedule an appointment, you may want to consider making a trip to just "drop by" the elected official's office. Preparation is always helpful in either case. If you plan to drop by an elected official's office, let the office know to expect your class and that you hope to meet with the legislator if he or she is available. Whether you have an appointment or not, send a fax or make a phone call several days before the trip, reminding the office of the class visit and presentation.

The down side to dropping by is that the class will likely not be able to see every legislator you've contacted. You should make plenty of contacts with your senators and representatives to increase the odds of catching those who are available to speak with the class. The down side to making appointments is the lack of flexibility. Being flexible is helpful as you maneuver a group of students through the capitol.

Debriefing

Following the meeting, talk with your students about how their lobbying effort went. What were some of the good points mentioned by the government official? What were some of the negative points? How did the meeting go? Do the students think they changed the person's mind? Is more work needed to change the person's mind? What did the students think of the experience? What would they do differently next time?

Follow-Up

After a visit or meeting, follow up with a letter of thanks for the meeting and a reminder of what was discussed. It's a good way to keep your issue and your position front and center. To make the point that advocacy doesn't end after the visit is over, allow the students to write follow-up letters.

Option to Making a Capitol Visit: Hosting a School Visit

Hosting an elected official at school is often easier than planning a field trip, but it is still helpful to have a game plan.

Consider taking the following steps as you plan to host a guest for a general meeting:

- Encourage the students to dress up for the occasion. Make the visit a big deal.
- Set up the space ahead of time. You will need chairs for the students and a special place for your guest to sit.
- Have one or two students greet your guest at the door and escort her or him to the meeting area.
- Welcome your guest and introduce her or him to the class. The students can be responsible for this, too.
- Proceed with the presentation.
- When the presentation is complete, allow your guest to respond before inviting the students to ask questions.
- Following the meeting make sure your guest is thanked for her or his time and escorted back to the main doors.
- Try to keep the meeting running on time out of respect for your guest's schedule and the schedule of the school day.

The format:

I. Opening prayer

II. Introduction of legislators and students

III. Stating the issue

IV. Research:
- What we have learned about our faith
- What we have learned about the issue

V. Testimonials by people affected by the issue

VI. Presentation of letters of support

VII. Response by legislators

VIII. Questions by students

IX. Conclusion

Possible Reactions to Advocacy

- Parents and/or parishioners may voice opposition to our issue.

    Taking a stand on social justice issues is often countercultural. Expect that there will be people, even practicing Catholics, who disagree on issues of social justice.

    Some people in your parish may think that church is not the place to discuss political issues. Because these situations arise, it is important that the position taken by the class, on any issue, is grounded in Catholic social teaching. If this is done, people can disagree with the advocacy, but you do have the backing of the Catholic Church.

    This is also a time when the support of the pastor is critical. Often, parishioners direct their disagreement to their pastor. A pastor knowledgeable about and supportive of the program can often defuse these situations.

- Partisanship may occur during the meeting with the government officials.

    The Catholic Church endorses no political party or specific representative or candidate. Rather, the Church supports positions based on its teachings. When dealing with legislators, however, sometimes political partisanship rears its head. For example, when meeting with one state representative, a Democrat, a student asked why he thought the bill the students were supporting wouldn't pass—as a Democrat had sponsored the bill. The legislator made a reply along these lines: Republicans are against the bill because they are out of touch with the people.

    In another example, following a meeting with a Republican congresswoman, an adult in the audience stood up and told the students that when they are old enough, they needed to vote for good Republicans like our guest.

    In both cases the partisanship was inappropriate. Partisanship can be difficult to deal with when it happens on the spot. Let your students know that as a Church, we don't look at politicians as being good or bad because they belong to one party or another. As Catholics, we are called to examine how our candidates stand on the issues and to vote by examining those values—Christian values—and our own consciences.

UNIT TWELVE

Doing Advocacy

Lesson 19: The Punch Line

Learning Objective

* The students will synthesize all the teachings of the *That's Not Fair* program.

The purpose of this activity is to help the students connect the messages taught throughout the program. The more connections they are able to make, the deeper the learning. The teacher can help the students expand on what the messages mean to our spiritual lives and the world around us.

Preparation

1. Prepare for the lesson by reviewing your notes made throughout the program and the key points of each activity:
* M&M's Game—charity and justice; people don't choose to be born into poverty and are sometimes unable to get out of poverty
* Creation—God creates all of us and wants all of us to live a decent life; all human persons are valuable; human persons can be easily damaged (from living in poverty)
* Preparing a Budget—it is difficult for many people to earn enough money to live a decent life
* Who Decides?—sometimes people in charge do not listen to those under them; people who are powerless feel frustrated when they are not listened to
* Loop Game—we are all connected; if we work together, we can help those who are less fortunate
* Jumping Through Ropes—some rules can make life more difficult than need be for those who are poor
* Illustrating the Issue—how a social justice issue affects those who live in poverty; how government officials can be lobbied to change their minds about an issue that affects those who are living in poverty; why social justice issues should be changed
* Explaining the Justice Issue—taking action on behalf of those who live in poverty is what God calls us to do
* Presentation to the Parish—making a case for change in policy and enlisting support from the community

The Lesson

1. Divide the class into teams of three or four students each.

2. Write on the chalkboard or marker board the names of the different activities completed throughout the program.
- M&M's Game
- Creation
- Preparing a Budget
- Who Decides?
- Loop Game
- Jumping Through Ropes
- Illustrating the Issue
- Explaining the Justice Issue
- Presentation to the Parish

3. Draw a circle around each activity.

4. Tell the students: "We're going to play a game. You have to make a connection between one activity and another. For example, we learned in 'Creation' that we are all made by God, and that is why we did an action for justice to help our brothers and sisters."

5. Draw a line from "Creation" to "Explaining the Justice Issue." Every time the students make a connection, you will draw a line.

6. Explain the rules of the game:
- One team at a time will give an example. We will go from team to team in order.
- You may not duplicate a line. That is, you may not make a connection already made by another team.
- You get a strike for not being able to come up with a connection or if you make a connection that does not make sense. (The teacher is the judge.) Each team gets two strikes. After two strikes your team is out.
- The last team "standing" wins the game.

7. Allow the students to start making connections. Make notes about their connections and their comments. You will need them for the final evaluation.

8. Once all the possible connections have been made, tie it together as much as possible with the students.

9. Hand out the evaluation form. Let them know they are not being graded on their answers. This activity is for you to learn what they have learned.

10. Give them some time to complete the form.

FINAL EVALUATION

Name: _____ Date: _____

Answer the following questions:

1. How are human persons made?

2. Why are human persons valuable?

3. Why should we help those people who live in poverty?

4. When you hear the words *poor person,* what picture comes to mind?

5. What was one message from the "Loop Game"?

6. What was one message from the "M&M's Game"?

7. What was one message from the "Who Decides?" (not enough chairs) game?

8. What is the difference between charity and justice?

9. What was one message from the "Jumping Through Ropes" game?

10. What is the connection between Mass and helping people who are poor?

11. What is the most important thing you have learned from this program?

APPENDIX A

Job Description for Outside Presenter
Classroom Presenter

Requirements

- Teach *That's Not Fair* curriculum to students, which includes approximately twelve classroom sessions of 45 minutes each. (If a school has its sixth grade divided up into several classrooms, sessions must be done with each classroom; that is, do not combine all classes together at one time.)
- Attend one parish presentation with students.
- Attend two "field trips": one to a social service agency and one to a government office or other agency.
- Attend training sessions.
- Complete the sessions within the designated time frame.

Length of Commitment

- One school year (October through March)

Skills and Traits Needed

- Some aptitude for teaching or communicating with children
- A desire to help those who are less fortunate
- An understanding of Catholic social teaching
- Flexible hours (negotiated between you and the teacher)
- Experience working with low-income persons or a background in social justice is a plus

Benefits

- Growing in your own faith as you share elements of the Catholic faith with young people
- The opportunity to make a difference in the lives of youth and in the lives of people who are in need
- The opportunity to be a voice for people who are in need in the systems that affect them
- A stipend

APPENDIX B

Sample Press Release for *That's Not Fair*

Contact Information
(Your name)
(Your address)
(Your e-mail address)

500 Young Students Get Jeff City's Attention—Legislators will come to KC to Listen to Students' Plea

(Kansas City, Missouri) Over 500 students from sixth, seventh, and eighth grade classes will hold a rally at 9:00 a.m. on Friday, March 14, at O'Hara High School, 9001 James A. Reed Road, to challenge state legislators to increase funding to the foster care system in the state of Missouri.

The students have been studying social justice in their schools since October, and now want to put what they have learned into practice. The students are from fifteen Catholic schools in the Kansas City area.

The students have learned that approximately 12,000 children are in the foster care system in our state. Last August, a two-year-old boy, Dominic James, was killed while in foster care in Springfield.

The students have met with foster parents and have heard first-hand about other deficiencies in the foster care system. Last year students met with Lieutenant Governor Joe Maxwell. He told them, "The foster care system in our state stinks!"

The students agree. Motivated by a desire to help children, these students will hold a rally and ask state legislators to increase funding for the foster care system.

Senators Ronnie DePasco and Charles Wheeler and Representatives John Burnett, Kate Meiners, Terry Young, Marsha Campbell, and Mike Sager have agreed to come to the rally. Others are expected; they're just not confirmed as yet.

The students will have collected thousands of signatures from qualified voters to support their effort. These will be presented at the rally.

The students will present a short video and PowerPoint presentation to help make their case. Cheerleaders and a school band will make it a lively rally. Don't miss it!

For more information about the rally, contact Lori Ross, executive director of Mid-America Foster Care and Adoption Association, at 816-350-0215, or Tom Turner, executive director of Bishop Sullivan Center, at 816-231-0984.

###

APPENDIX C

Pastor Packet: Sample Letters
Beginning of Year Letter to Pastors

Dear _____,

This coming school year, the sixth grade students in your school, plus those in twenty-one other schools in our diocese, will be using the *That's Not Fair* program to teach them about Catholic social doctrine. The course ends with the students performing some act of advocacy vis-à-vis a legislative body.

Last year the issue the students advocated for was on behalf of the children with special needs who are waiting for adoption in the state of Missouri. There are approximately 1,200 children (not infants) bouncing around foster homes waiting to be adopted. The students asked the state of Missouri to create a media campaign to recruit more adoptive parents. The best prevention of poverty is a stable home, which so many children right now do not enjoy.

This year we plan to work on this same issue, as we did not get what we wanted last year.

At the end of the program last year, we conducted an evaluation session with the teachers. Overall, they were very positive about the program and were glad to see their students learn about Catholic social doctrine and how to put it into practice.

The teachers' one lament was that they wished the people in their parish would have been more involved with the students and this issue. We told them we need the support of the pastors to really make that happen.

That's why we are writing to you.

We know you have a zillion things on your plate, but we are asking you to consider having a zillion and one. We would really appreciate it if you could come to a meeting on August 12, 10:30 a.m., at Saint Patrick's (North Kansas City), as we describe in more detail the issue and our strategy for advocacy for the students in your school this coming year.

Last year we held a rally of five hundred students at O'Hara High School, and ten legislators from Jefferson City came. Four pastors came as well. We're hoping more of you can be part of this year's rally.

We've enclosed an RSVP card. If you can't make it to this meeting, we would be willing to meet with you at your convenience sometime this fall to discuss this issue with you.

Thanks for all you do.

Sincerely yours,

Thomas Turner and Neal Colby
Director, Bishop Sullivan Center, and Diocesan Director of Social Concerns
cc: Bishop Boland

Pastor's Letter to Legislator

Dear _____,

During the school year the students in our middle school have been studying how their faith relates to issues in the "public square." Our students have been learning about the foster care system in our state. They believe there is a need for improvement in this system.

Our students, along with students from seventeen other schools in our diocese, will be holding a rally on Friday, March 14, 9:00 a.m., at O'Hara High School. The rally will last about an hour. During the rally the students will present testimony from foster care parents about where they hope improvement can be made in the foster care system.

As our representative, I sure hope you can attend this rally.

Letter to Pastors About Rally

Dear _____,

This past year your school has participated in our *That's Not Fair* program, which teaches middle school students about Catholic social doctrine. Seventeen other schools in our diocese, as well as many schools in St. Louis, Missouri, likewise participated in this program.

The program culminates with the students advocating vis-à-vis a group of legislators over some issue that is on the Missouri Catholic Conference's agenda. The issue the students will advocate for this year is to improve the foster care system in our state. This system is grossly underfunded and undermanaged and is in need of repair. It is putting many children in the system at risk.

The Kansas City–St. Joseph diocesan students will conduct a large rally on Friday, March 14, 9:00 a.m., at O'Hara High School. They will meet with as many state legislators as possible. Last year, ten KC-area legislators attended the rally. The St. Louis students will hold a similar rally with their legislators on March 7.

I have enclosed for you an explanation of the issue and a sample letter that you may want to include in your bulletin the week before your students make a presentation at your weekend Masses. The purpose of the student presentation is to educate the adults in the parish and to collect signatures to be turned in at the rally. The teachers should handle all of this for you.

Obviously, I hope you will attend the rally on March 14. It will last about an hour and will be followed by Mass at Saint Regis. Last year five hundred students attended.

If you have questions about any of this, please call me at [816-231-0984] or e-mail me at [*tturner@bishopsullivan.org*].

Sincerely yours,
Thomas Turner, director
cc:

APPENDIX D
Rally Packet

Rally procedure

1. Opening prayer

2. Welcome and introduction of legislators

3. Introduction of schools

4. Stating the purpose of the rally: asking legislators to provide more assistance to kids in foster care

5. PowerPoint presentation by two students, briefly describing the key values they learned through their social justice program

6. Holding up symbols of children

7. PowerPoint presentation by two students, giving the results of their research about the foster care system in the state of Missouri

8. Testimonies from two or three foster parents

9. Presentations to the legislators of letters of support the students have gathered from voting adults

10. Students request of legislators given by way of four-minute video

11. Legislators respond to students' request and research

12. Panel of three students ask follow-up questions of legislators

13. Expression of gratitude by students to legislators

14. Adjournment

Rally Flyer Sent to Legislators

500 Young Students to Hold Rally with Their State Legislators

Over 500 students from fourteen schools throughout the Kansas City Metro area will hold a rally on Friday, March 14, at 9:00 a.m., at O'Hara High School, 9001 James A. Reed Road, to ask Missouri legis-

lators to do whatever they can to improve the foster care system in our state.

The students have been studying social justice in their schools since October, and now want to put what they have learned into practice.

They have met with foster care parents and listened to their stories. They have researched the foster care system in our state. They learned that the system is understaffed and has suffered budget cuts the past few years. The ones who lose the most with budget cuts are the kids in foster care.

They will present their case to legislators by way of a PowerPoint presentation and video in a controlled rally. After presenting their research, they will ask the legislators to respond. They have collected over 5,000 signatures from adults in support of their efforts.

This will be the second year that students have held such a rally. Those legislators who attended last year found it to be a positive experience. They appreciated seeing so many young people interested in government.

If you can attend, please let Tom Turner, coordinator of the program, know. He can be reached at 816-231-0984 or by e-mail at *tturner@bishopsullivan.org*. The rally will start promptly at 9:00 a.m. and last no more than an hour.

So far, Senator DePasco and Representatives Burnett, Campbell, Meiners, and Sager have agreed to attend.

Script for Rally

(Two students serve as emcees.)

9:00 Introduction and opening prayer
Good morning, and welcome. My name is _____, and this is _____. We are in the _____ grade at Saint Patrick School. Let us begin by praying together the Lord's Prayer: Our Father . . .

9:02 Introduction of guests
I want to welcome our special guests: Senators Ronnie DePasco and Charles Wheeler and Representatives John Burnett, Kate Meiners, Marsha Campbell, Terry Young, and Mike Sager.

9:03 Introduction of schools
We thank you for coming to our rally. We represent fourteen Catholic schools. When I call out the name of your school, please stand and remain standing until I have called all the schools' names: St. Therese, St. Peter, St. Charles, St. Patrick, St. James, St. Gabriel, Visitation, St. Stephen, Nativity, St. Elizabeth, St. Thomas More, St. Regis, St. John LaLande, Our Lady of Lourdes.

You may be seated.

9:05 Stating the issue

Fellow students, often the only time we get together is when we are opponents in different sports. But today we come together as one team, fighting for a common cause.

Senators and representatives, we have come here today on behalf of other children in the state of Missouri—some of them the same age as us—who are in foster care. We have all met with foster care parents in our classrooms. We have learned that the foster care system in our state is not working very well, and we are hoping you will do whatever you can to FIX IT. We are hoping you will do whatever you can to HELP THESE KIDS.

(Cheerleaders lead chant: "Help these kids!")

For the past four months, we have learned some important values that our Church teaches and we have learned about the foster care system in our state. First, we would like to take a few minutes to let you know what we have learned, and then we have some questions for all of you.

9:10 Research (two students give research)

We have been studying the Catholic Church's teaching on social justice since last October. _____ from (school) and _____ from (school), will tell you what we have learned.

9:11 PowerPoint presentation

Through an activity we call the "M&M's Game," we learned several things:
- Some people have more than others.
- People who have less need help.
- One way to help people in need, like kids in foster care, is to change the rules to help them.

Through an activity we call "Creation," we have learned:
- All people were created by God.
- Each person is a child of God.
- Therefore, every person has the right to a decent life.

Through an activity called "Who Decides?," we have learned:
- People who do not have enough power often don't have their needs heard.
- It is important that everyone's voice be heard.
- We are here today as the voice of the 12,000 kids in our state who are in foster care.

Through an activity called "Loop Game," we have learned:
- Because we are all created by God, we are connected to one another.
- Because we are connected, we are responsible for one another.
- We are especially responsible for those who fall behind in society.

Through this whole program, we have learned:
- It is important for us to apply our beliefs and values to problems in society.

Emcee: Thank you for this presentation.

9:16 Holding up of symbols

We have been learning about the needs of children in our state who are in foster care. There are about 12,000 children in our state in foster care; that's a lot of kids. We made up symbols for these children. I now ask all the students to please hold up the symbols. This represents only about 10 percent of all those in foster care. There are many more. Foster parents and social workers are doing all they can to help these kids, but they need your support.

(Cheerleaders lead chant: "Give them help!")

9:19 More research (PowerPoint presentation: three students give research)

Here are some things we have learned:

First, we learned some good news. Last year we held a rally like this to ask legislators to help increase funding for an adoption awareness law. We learned that Representative Mike Sager has introduced a bill to do that this year. We want to thank Representative Sager for doing this. Let's give him a special cheer of "Thank you, Mike."

(Cheerleaders lead chant: "Thank you, Mike!")

We learned that the state of Missouri is near the bottom of all the states in our country in what it pays foster parents.

Over the past few years, the state of Missouri has taken away money for training classes for people who are willing to become foster parents.

The state has taken away money to reimburse foster parents for medication they buy kids in their care and has taken away money to reimburse them for using their cars to take foster kids to important appointments.

Last August, Dominic James, a two-year-old boy, was killed while in foster care. Because there are too few social workers, they cannot keep up with all their cases. Dominic's father told the Division of Family Services, "Before you admit a flaw in children's services, you'll let my son die."

After the death of Dominic James, Governor Holden ordered an investigation of the foster care system. This investigation said that social workers have too many kids they are looking after and that their caseloads need to be reduced to no more than twenty-five per worker.

Recently, a judge has ruled that Missouri's system for paying foster care providers violates federal law because it fails to consider basic costs for the children, such as food, clothing, and school supplies.

We recently learned that legislators are considering taking away all the money that provides health insurance for children in low-income homes, many of whom end up in foster care. This would be a tragedy if you do this.

Last year a group of us met with Lieutenant Governor Joe Maxwell. He told us, "The foster care system in the state of Missouri stinks."

Governor Holden said about the foster care system: "Public confidence must be restored in the system. Every child in Missouri is entitled to a safe place to live. That's a right, not a privilege."

After learning about the foster care system, we agree. And that's why we want you to do what you can to HELP THESE KIDS.

(Cheerleaders lead chant: "Help these kids!")

9:22 Introduction of foster parent

We are honored to have many foster care parents with us this morning. We would like them to stand, and let's show them our thanks by our applause. We have asked _____ to say a few words on their behalf.

9:30 Presentation of letters of support

We know that you know that none of us can vote. But our parents and other adults in our parish can. So we told them about this issue and that we were going to meet with you this morning. We collected letters from adults in our parishes, asking you to do more to help kids in foster care.

I would now ask my fellow students to bring forward letters from your parishes and schools, signed by adults who vote, to let our legislative leaders know how many people support our effort. (One or two students from each school present the letters.)

(Cheerleaders lead chant: "Help these kids!")

9:35 Students' request and legislators' response

We'd like to show now, by way of video, what we want for the foster care system and why we want it. (Run the video.)

Thank you for listening to us; now it's our turn to listen to you. What can the state do to do a better job of helping kids in foster care?

Legislators respond.

9:46 Student questions (from a three-student panel)

Some students would like to ask a few follow-up questions:

- How would you feel if one of your kids was in our state's foster care system?
- What's more important in our state than taking care of kids who are in trouble?
- Do you take us seriously, or do you see us as just a bunch of kids?
- After this rally, will you personally do something in Jefferson City to help kids in foster care?
- Last year our schoolmates asked the legislators to write our schools a letter so we would know if you did anything to help us. Although everyone said they would write us a letter, only two did. Will any of you be willing to follow up with our schools and parishes with a letter so we know what you did?

After the student questions:

We want to thank you for coming this morning and listening to us. We appreciate anything you can do to help the kids in foster care.

We have a gift for each one of you. It is a special cup. In the Gospel of Matthew, Jesus says, "Whoever gives only a cup of cold water to one of these little ones to drink . . . , he will surely not lose his reward" (10:42). We are giving you a cup to remind you to do whatever you can for kids in foster care. Those kids represent the "little ones" Jesus speaks of, and they need much more than cold water. (Have different students present cups to each legislator.)

Let us show the legislators our appreciation for them coming here this morning.

10:00 Conclusion

This concludes our rally.

We will exit through these doors and attend Mass at Saint Regis Church next door to ask God to look after these children.

APPENDIX E

Recommended Sources for Further Reading

Foundational Sources

Compendium of the Social Doctrine of the Church. Rome: Pontifical Council for Justice and Peace, Libreria Editrice Vaticana, 2004. English translation, United States Conference of Catholic Bishops, 2005.

O'Brien, David, and Thomas A. Shannon, eds. *Catholic Social Thought: The Documentary Heritage.* Maryknoll, NY: Orbis Books, 1997. One-volume compendium of the major teachings of the Church on social justice.

Introductory Sources

Charles, Rodger. *An Introduction to Catholic Social Teaching.* San Francisco: Ignatius Press, 2000.

Himes, Kenneth R. *Responses to 101 Questions on Catholic Social Teaching.* Mahwah, NJ: Paulist Press, 2001.

Massaro, Thomas. *Living Justice: Catholic Social Teaching in Action.* Lanham, MD: Sheed and Ward, 2000.

More Advanced Sources

Curran, Charles E. *Catholic Social Teaching: A Historical, Theological, and Ethical Analysis.* Washington, DC: Georgetown University Press, 2002.

Dorr, Donal. *Option for the Poor: 100 years of Catholic Teaching.* Revised ed. Dublin, Ireland: Gill and MacMillan, 1992.

———. *Spirituality and Justice.* Maryknoll, NY: Orbis Books, 1985.

Himes, Michael J. and Kenneth R. *Fullness of Faith: The Public Significance of Theology.* Mahwah, NJ: Paulist Press, 1993.

Hobgood, Mary. *Catholic Social Teaching and Economic Theory: Paradigms in Conflict.* Philadelphia: Temple University Press, 1991.

Mich, Marvin L. Krier. *Catholic Social Teaching and Movements.* Mystic, CT: Twenty-Third Publications, 1998.

Schuck, Michael J. *That They Be One: The Social Teaching of the Papal Encyclicals, 1740–1989.* Washington, DC: Georgetown University Press, 1991.

ACKNOWLEDGMENTS

The scriptural quotations in this book are from the New American Bible with Revised New Testament and Revised Psalms. Copyright © 1991, 1986, and 1970 by the Confraternity of Christian Doctrine, Washington, D.C. Used by the permission of the copyright owner. All rights reserved. No part of the New American Bible may be reproduced in any form without permission in writing from the copyright owner.

The seven principles on pages 11–13 are summarized from *Sharing Catholic Social Teaching: Challenges and Directions,* by the United States Conference of Catholic Bishops (USCCB), pages 4–6, at *www.nccbuscc.org/sdwp/projects/socialteaching.htm,* accessed October 19 2005.

The quotations by the USCCB on pages 18, 19, 29, 40, and 40, handout 5, and pages 55 and 63 are from *Economic Justice for All: Pastoral Letter on Catholic Social Teaching and the U.S. Economy,* by the USCCB, 1986, numbers 120, 39, 28, 337, 86, 337, 86, 124, and 365, respectively, at *www.osjspm.org/cst/eja.htm,* accessed October 19, 2005.

The quotations by Pope Paul VI on pages 19–20, 28–29, and 40 handout 5, and page 81 are from "Pastoral Constitution on the Church in the Modern World *Gaudium et Spes* Promulgated by His Holiness, Pope Paul VI," on December 7, 1965, numbers 30, 27, 31, 31, and 4, respectively, at *www.vatican.va/archive/hist_councils/ii_vatican_council/documents/vat-ii_cons_19651207_gaudium-et-spes_en.html,* accessed October 19, 2005.

The quotation on page 19 is from *Justice in the World,* by the World Synod of Catholic Bishops, 1971, number 34, at *www.osjspm.org/cst/jw.htm,* accessed October 19, 2005.

The quotations by Pope John Paul II on pages 19, 29, and 40 handout 5, and page 54–55 are from *"Centesimus Annus,* The Hundredth Year," 1991, numbers 49, 11, 29, 29, and 48, respectively, at *www.osjspm.org/cst/ca.htm,* accessed October 19, 2005.

The excerpt on page 27 is from the English translation of the *Catechism of the Catholic Church* for use in the United States of America, number 1703. Copyright © 1994 by the United States Catholic Conference, Inc.—Libreria Editrice Vaticana. Used with permission.

The quotation from the USCCB on pages 29 and 40 and handout 5 is from *The Challenge of Peace: God's Promise and Our Response,* part 1, 1983, numbers 15, 15, and 15, at *www.osjspm.org/cst/cp.htm,* accessed October 24, 2005.

The quotations on pages 40 and 40, handout 5, and page 68 are from or adapted from *"Rerum Novarum* Encyclical of Pope Leo XIII on Capital and Labor,"* numbers 22, 34, 22, 22, and 35, respectively, at *www.vatican.va/holy_father/leo_xiii/encyclicals/documents/hf_l-xiii_enc_15051891_rerum-novarum_en.html,* accessed October 24, 2005.

The quotations on page 40, handout 5, and page 69 are adapted from *"Pacem in Terris* Encyclical of Pope John XXIII on Establishing Universal Peace in Truth, Justice, Charity, and Liberty,"* numbers 64, 64, and 37, respectively, at *www.vatican.va/holy_father/john_xxiii/encyclicals/documents/hf_j-xxiii_enc_11041963_pacem_en.html,* accessed October 24, 2005.

The quotations on page 41, handout 5, and pages 64 and 81 are adapted from *"Populorum Progressio* Encyclical of Pope Paul VI on the Development of Peoples,"* numbers 35, 35, 17, and 81, respectively, at *www.vatican.va/holy_father/paul_vi/encyclicals/documents/hf_p-vi_enc_26031967_populorum_en.html,* accessed October 24, 2005.

The quotations on handout 5 and on pages 64, 68, and 81 are quoted or adapted from *"Mater et Magistra* Encyclical of Pope John XXIII on Christianity and Social Progress,"* numbers 3, 157, 38, and 257, respectively, at *www.vatican.va/holy_father/john_xxiii/encyclicals/documents/hf_j-xxiii_enc_15051961_mater_en.html,* accessed October 24, 2005.

The quotations on handout 5 and page 69 are from or adapted from *"Laborem Exercens,"* by Pope John Paul II, numbers 19 and 24, at *www.vatican.va/edocs/ENG0217/__PP.HTM,* accessed October 24, 2005.

The quotations on pages 54 and 68 are from *"Quadragesimo Anno* Encyclical of Pope Pius XI on Reconstruction of the Social Order . . . ,"* numbers 79 and 136, at *www.vatican.va/holy_father/pius_xi/encyclicals/documents/hf_p-xi_enc_19310515_quadragesimo-anno_en.html,* accessed October 24, 2005.

The quotations on pages 63, 64, 64, and 69 are from *"Sollicitudo Rei Socialis,"* by Pope John Paul II, numbers 38, 40, 39, and 16, respectively, at *www.vatican.va/edocs/ENG0223/_INDEX.HTM,* accessed October 24, 2005.

To view copyright terms and conditions for Internet materials cited here, log on to the home pages for the referenced Web sites.

During this book's preparation, all citations, facts, figures, names, addresses, telephone numbers, Internet URLs, and other pieces of information cited within were verified for accuracy. The authors and Saint Mary's Press staff have made every attempt to reference current and valid sources, but we cannot guarantee the content of any source, and we are not responsible for any changes that may have occurred since our verification. If you find an error in, or have a question or concern about, any of the information or sources listed within, please contact Saint Mary's Press.

Endnotes Cited in Quotations from Documents Copyrighted by the USCCB and The Holy See

1. France adopted a "family" or "children's" allowance in 1932, followed by Italy in 1936, The Netherlands in 1939, The United Kingdom in 1945, and Sweden in 1947. Arnold Heidenheimer, Hugh Heclo, and Carolyn Teich Adams, *Comparative Public Policy: The Politics of Social Choice in Europe and America* (New York: St. Martin's Press, 1975), 189, 199. See also Robert Kuttner, *The Economic Illusion* (Boston: Houghton Mifflin Company, 1984) 243–247; and Joseph Picciones, *Help for Families on the Front Lines: The Theory and Practice of Family Allowances* (Washington, DC: The Free Congress Research and Education Foundation, 1983).

2. J. Alfaro, "Theology of Justice in the World" (Rome: Pontifical Commission on Justice and Peace, 1973), 40–41; E. McDonagh, "The Making of Disciples" (Wilmington, DE: Michael Glazier, 1982), 119.

3. *Gaudium et spes* 24 § 3.

4. Cf. *Matt.* 24:13; 13:24–30 and 36–43.

5. Cf. *2 Cor.* 6:10.

6. Second Vatican Ecumenical Council, Pastoral Constitution on the Church in the World of Today *Gaudium et Spes*, 24.

7. Ibid., q. xxxii, a. 6, Answer.

8. Pius XI, Encyclical Letter *Quadragesimo Anno*, I : *loc. cit.*, 184–186.

9. Irma T. Elo and Calvin L. Baele, *Rural Development, Poverty, and Natural Resources* (Washington, DC: National Center for Food and Agriculture Policy, Resources for Future, 1985).